GCSE Music
Study Guide

AQA

Richard Knight

R·

Rhinegold Education

239–241 Shaftesbury Avenue
London WC2I1 8TF
Telephone: 020 7333 1720
Fax: 020 7333 1765

www.rhinegold.co.uk

Music Study Guides

GCSE, AS and A2 Music Study Guides (AQA, Edexcel and OCR)
GCSE, AS and A2 Music Listening Tests (AQA, Edexcel and OCR)
GCSE Music Study Guide (WJEC)
GCSE Music Listening Tests (WJEC)
AS/A2 Music Technology Study Guide (Edexcel)
AS/A2 Music Technology Listening Tests (Edexcel)
Revision Guides for GCSE (AQA, Edexcel and OCR), AS and A2 Music (AQA and Edexcel)

Also available from Rhinegold Education

Key Stage 3 Elements
Key Stage 3 Listening Tests: Book 1 and Book 2
AS and A2 Music Harmony Workbooks
GCSE and AS Music Composition Workbooks
GCSE and AS Music Literacy Workbooks
Romanticism in Focus, Baroque Music in Focus, Film Music in Focus, Modernism in Focus,
The Immaculate Collection in Focus, *Who's Next* in Focus, *Batman* in Focus, *Goldfinger* in Focus,
Musicals in Focus

Rhinegold also publishes Choir & Organ, Classical Music, Classroom Music, Early Music Today,
International Piano, Music Teacher, Opera Now, Piano, The Singer, Teaching Drama,
British and International Music Yearbook, British Performing Arts Yearbook, British Music Education Yearbook,
Rhinegold Dictionary of Music in Sound

Other Rhinegold Study Guides

Rhinegold publishes resources for candidates studying Drama and Theatre Studies.

First published 2009 in Great Britain by
Rhinegold Publishing Limited
239–241 Shaftesbury Avenue
London WC2H 8TF
Telephone: 020 7333 1720
Fax: 020 7333 1765
www.rhinegold.co.uk

You should always check the current requirements of the examination, since these may change.
Copies of the AQA Specification can be downloaded from the AQA website at www.aqa.org.uk or may be
purchased from AQA publications, Unit Two, Wheel Forge Way, Trafford Park, Manchester M17 1EH.
Telephone: 0870 410 1036 Fax: 0161 953 1177 Email: publications@aqa.org.uk

AQA GCSE Music Study Guide
British Library Cataloguing in Publication Data.
A catalogue record for this book is available from the British Library.
ISBN 978-1-906178-79-6
Printed in Great Britain by Headley Brothers Ltd

CONTENTS

THE AUTHOR

Richard Knight read music at St John's College, Oxford, and has been director of music at two leading independent schools. He now combines teaching with work as a principal examiner at A level and is on the panel of examiners for the ABRSM. Richard is one of the authors of *Elements: The Rhinegold Guide to Key Stage 3 Music* and a frequent contributor to *Classroom Music*. He also presents conferences for students and teachers. As a composer, he has a large catalogue of works to his name, including the oratorio *The Crown of Life*, a classroom musical *The King of Ireland's Son*, and various orchestral and chamber works. Richard has a particular interest in all things South American and is also an inland waterways enthusiast.

ACKNOWLEDGEMENTS

The author would like to thank the consultant Chris Cook, and the Rhinegold editorial and design team of Matthew Hammond, Katherine Smith, Lucien Jenkins and Silvia Schreiber for their expert support in the preparation of this book.

The author and publishers are grateful to the following publishers for permission to use printed excerpts from their publications:

Edelweiss, words and music by Oscar Hammerstein II and Richard Rodgers. © 1959, reproduced by permission of EMI Music Publishing Ltd., London W8 5SW.

On the Street where You Live. Words by Alan Jay Lerner, music by Frederick Loewe. © 1956 Chappell & Co Inc., Warner/Chappell North America Ltd. Reproduced by permission of Faber Music Ltd. All rights reserved.

Luck Be A Lady. Words & Music by Frank Loesser, © Copyright 1950 (Renewed 1978) Frank Music Corporation, USA. MPL Communications Limited. Used by Permission of Music Sales Limited. All Rights Reserved. International Copyright Secured.

Didi. Words and Music by Khaled Hadj Brahim. © 1992 EMI Music Publishing France. EMI Music Publishing Ltd. Reproduced by permission of International Music Publications Ltd (a trading name of Faber Music Ltd). All Rights Reserved.

Cover photograph of John Lee Hooker by Al Pereira/Michael Ochs Archives/Getty Images.

WHY STUDY MUSIC?

So you are just about to start on a GCSE course in Music: what can you expect to gain from your studies between now and the day you take the final exam?

Most people like to listen to music: maybe for relaxation or entertainment, to create an appropriate atmosphere at a party or in a restaurant, or to express emotions in certain circumstances (for example, in a cinema or at a wedding).

This inner instinct to respond to music is almost universal, yet, for many people, it never develops into a trained skill; nor are they able to use their musical appreciation in a practical way to express their own personality and emotions through the performance of music or the composing of their own music. They just continue to enjoy the sound of the music that they know they like to listen to.

At GCSE you will study music in much greater depth than you will have done in school up to this point. The further you develop your understanding of the vast world of music from around the planet and across the centuries the more accessible more music becomes to you. In particular:

- You will be aware of more happening in the music you like to listen to: instead of just hearing the melody, the lyrics or the drum beat, you will hear some of the subtleties in the rhythm, the harmony and the instrumentation
- You will become aware of more styles of music and understand what music of different styles is expressing; this will lead to a wider and richer selection of music that you like to listen to
- You will be more informed about how to perform music to bring out the full effect of a piece or song
- You will improve your instinct for how notes can be made to fit together to create a wide range of musical effects; this will give you more confidence for improvising and composing your own music.

If this sounds good to you, then you will find much to enjoy over your GCSE course. This may well be the start of a long adventure exploring the world's musical traditions and developing your skills as a musician.

ABOUT THE COURSE

There are three different exam boards in England that offer a GCSE in Music. This study guide is written to match with the AQA course which will be first examined in June 2011. There are **four units**:

Unit 1: Listening to and Appraising Music	20% of the marks
Unit 2: Composing and Appraising Music	20% of the marks
Unit 3: Performing Music	40% of the marks
Unit 4: Composing Music	20% of the marks

This structure means that 40% of your GCSE marks are for your performing skills, 30% for your listening and appraising skills, and 30% for your composing skills.

There are some other key terms that AQA use to explain their course: 'Area of Study' and 'Strand'.

There are **five Areas of Study**:

Rhythm and Metre	(Area of Study 1)
Harmony and Tonality	(Area of Study 2)
Texture and Melody	(Area of Study 3)
Timbre and Dynamics	(Area of Study 4)
Structure and Form	(Area of Study 5)

These terms are sometimes called the Elements of Music; they may be familiar to you from your Key Stage 3 work in music.

There are **three Strands**:

- The Western Classical Tradition
- Popular Music of the 20th and 21st centuries
- World Music.

In order to steer a successful path through the AQA specification, it is important that you know what the terms 'Unit', 'Area of Study' and 'Strand' mean.

ABOUT THIS BOOK

This book is intended to help students prepare for AQA's examination in GCSE Music. The aim is to provide:

- Explanation of the technical terms and features that you are expected to know for each **Area of Study**
- An introduction to the music found in each **Strand**
- Advice on how to prepare for the demands of each **Unit** to give you the best possible chance of obtaining the marks available.

Use this book to look up various technical points you are unclear about, to remind yourself about musical topics that you meet for the first time in class, and to refresh your mind over the best way to approach each of the units in the examination.

HOW YOU CAN HELP YOURSELF

LISTENING

Most students take two years to cover the GCSE course, and this will allow your teacher time to work through the content of the AQA course, but do not put all the responsibility for the development of your musical skills on your teacher's shoulders.

The classroom is an obvious place to learn about music, and your teacher will no doubt be doing his or her best to train you in all the requirements of the GCSE specification; however, it is not always the best way of learning about music. Music is a special form of art that comes to life only when it is performed. The theory of why one particular musical feature achieves the effect it does is valuable, but it only really makes sense when it is heard. A good way, therefore, to help yourself make good progress, is to listen to music regularly.

Listening is a skill. This means it is not the same as hearing, which we do involuntarily whenever there is a noise within earshot. You can have music playing and quickly find that all you are doing is hearing it while your brain focuses on something else: texting, reading, doing your homework, or just letting your mind relax. Listening means that your brain focuses on the noise reaching your ears as you try to understand what is going on in all the various layers that make up a piece of music. There is nothing wrong with having music on in the background, but try to establish the habit of really listening to some music regularly.

A second dimension to a good listening habit is to vary your diet: don't always listen to your favourite song, band, or style of the moment. Explore the various styles that are available on different radio stations, try downloading something different than usual onto your MP3 player, or try borrowing some CDs from a library of music that you haven't listened to before. Best of all, find out what music is on live in your area and ask someone to take you to some live performances. Most styles of music really are best when heard live, since the experience of what you are hearing is magnified by being able to watch the musicians, and by the atmosphere in the venue.

PLAYING

Even more beneficial than regular listening to music is regular playing of music. There is, of course, a direct value to the GCSE course since Unit 3 requires you to perform (and you will recall that this unit is worth 40% of the marks); however, the benefit is much more significant than this one aspect of GCSE music. By developing your playing skills you will get to experience music from the inside: the theoretical stuff that can seem very dry and dull in the classroom and is easily forgotten when listening to the wonderful overall effect of a piece of music, soon becomes an instinctive understanding when you are playing music yourself. Not sure what effect compound time signatures create? Play some music in your school orchestra that is in $\frac{6}{8}$ and you will soon be picking up the feel of music in this metre. Not certain what a riff is? You'll soon know when you play in a band.

So, make sure you are involved in some regular music-making over the two years that you are studying for your Music GCSE: practise your instrument(s) often, and join a choir, orchestra or band. You will probably soon find that music becomes a favourite part of your weekly routine, something that seems rather different to other subjects you are taking.

COMPOSING

Two of the four GCSE units require you to compose your own music. You may already have experience of inventing your own music – either in the work you have done in class, or through improvising with the instrument you play, perhaps in a band. Composing music can be a fascinating and rewarding musical activity, but it can also be daunting: just how are you going to fill two minutes with music? Like all musical skills this needs to be practised. Just as you wouldn't like to perform in public after a long period of never playing your instrument, so you shouldn't expect to compose your final pieces without developing a habit of inventing and developing musical ideas.

So each time you are practising your instrument, before you pack up, try to make up a short piece of music. Set yourself small challenges to awaken your musical imagination. Try to play music that represents different moods, or colours, or animals, or times of day, or types of weather. Also, try to explore different shapes or parts of your instrument's capabilities: shapes that leap, or fall, or use repeated notes, or are based in the lowest register, or contrast extremes of dynamics. All this will help to build your self-confidence and imagination for composing. These are very valuable attributes but cannot be developed in a single week, so start the habit now!

SUMMARY

You have chosen a fantastic subject to study at GCSE. Music is one of the most rewarding of pursuits, and you will find much to enjoy if you come to it with a spirit of curiosity, open-mindedness and willingness to share other people's music-making. Good luck!

As part of the GCSE specification, AQA have prepared a list of musical features and technical terms which they expect you to know and understand. This chapter of the book works through this musical vocabulary and explains each term, telling you what to listen out for.

RHYTHM AND METRE

PULSE

The vast majority of music is built on a **pulse**: a regularly occurring sense of beat in the music.

There is no coincidence that the words beat and pulse also relate to what the human heart does to keep us alive. Almost certainly, you will have had the experience of having had your pulse taken: it is a measure of your heartbeat, and confirms that you are alive!

In a similar way, for a piece of music to come to life and progress from its start to its finish, it needs to move from one beat to the next. In the vast majority of music this movement continues at a regular interval throughout the piece: perhaps one beat every second, for example. This creates a sense of pulse.

> When you find yourself tapping your foot to music, or clapping 'in time' with a song, perhaps in a stage musical, you are almost certainly copying the pulse of the music.

TEMPO

Tempo is the musician's word for speed, and, in particular, the speed that the pulse of the music is beating.

This is one of the most fundamental ways in which music can express the various moods and states of mind which we humans experience. The pulse of our heartbeat will vary according to mood: when we're feeling tranquil, sleepy, sad, or depressed it will be slow; when we feel excited, joyful, or angry it will be fast. By and large, music that expresses these moods follows the same principle.

The speed of music is usually defined by beats per minute: similar to the figure a nurse will record for our own pulse. It is almost certainly no coincidence that most music shares the same range of the human pulse between around 40 beats per minute (the heart-rate of a very fit person at rest) and up towards 200 beats per minute (the heart-rate of someone in the most intense exercise or crisis).

Sometimes composers will give a precise beat-per-minute value for their music. This is particularly significant in music for film or television, which has to match moving pictures perfectly. However, sometimes they just describe the required tempo in more general terms using a word.

> Try choosing scenes from your favourite films that capture these moods and listening carefully to the background music. How many beats per minute is the music accompanying each mood?

The language used for this is traditionally Italian, and you should be aware of the following words:

Italian Term	English meaning	Approx. range of BPM
Grave	Heavy or serious	40–60
Largo	Slow and broad	50–66
Lento	Slow	60–66
Andante	Walking pace	66–72
Moderato	Moderate speed	72–84
Allegretto	Quite lively and light-hearted	76–96
Allegro	Lively or cheerful	96–120
Vivace	Full of life	110–140
Presto	Fast	140–180
Prestissimo	Very fast	180–210

 Exercise 1

For each of the following moods in the left hand column, choose which tempo you think would best suit a piece of music that was trying to capture that mood. Give an Italian term and a likely beats-per-minute figure.

Mood	Tempo marking (Italian)	Suggested BPM
Angry		
Content		
Excited		
Depressed		
Happy		
Tired		

NOTE VALUES

We measure how long each note lasts by counting the number of beats that pass by between the moment the note is first played and the moment that it stops.

One of the most important aspects of musical notation is the part that shows this information. Note length is shown by a combination of the notehead (is it filled in or empty?) and the presence/absence of a stem or tail. These are shown on the chart below and if these are still unfamiliar to you as you start your GCSE course, it should be a priority to learn them now. The American names of the notes are also given here, as these will help in understanding time signatures.

Number of beats	Note symbol	Rest symbol	English name	American name
4	𝅝	—	Semibreve	Whole note
2	𝅗𝅥	—	Minim	Half note
1	𝅘𝅥	𝄽	Crotchet	Quarter note
½	𝅘𝅥𝅮	𝄾	Quaver	Eighth note
¼	𝅘𝅥𝅯	𝄿	Semiquaver	Sixteenth note
⅛	𝅘𝅥𝅰	𝅀	Demisemiquaver	Thirty-second note

You may notice that the English name for the four-beat note starts with 'semi-', which suggests it is half of something bigger. Well, there is one even longer note value which is eight beats long and called a breve (𝄺). These notes were used many centuries ago in the Renaissance period, but are now quite rare. You are unlikely to come across one at GCSE.

You may be wondering what happens for a note lasting three beats. We have two options for this. You can use a minim and a crotchet and join them together using a gently curving line called a **tie**. Alternatively, and more commonly, you can write a minim and put a **dot** after the note; this indicates you add on half of the note's value. So a minim is worth two beats, but by having a dot after the note you add on an extra half of those two beats, giving you a total of three beats. Rests can also be 'dotted' in the same way.

Exercise 2

If you are new to this kind of notation, look at the following line of notes, or tune, and write underneath each note how many beats each note lasts for:

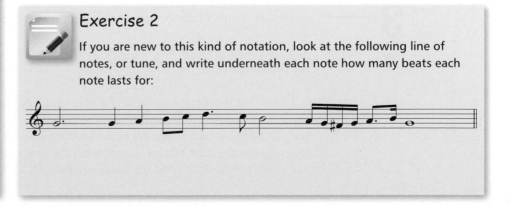

METRE

You will be used to measuring the size of things in metres. In music, metre is also a way of measuring out the beats in a piece.

If you look at your metre ruler, you will probably see each millimetre is indicated, but that after every 10th millimetre there is a mark of greater significance: this is where we have reached the next centimetre.

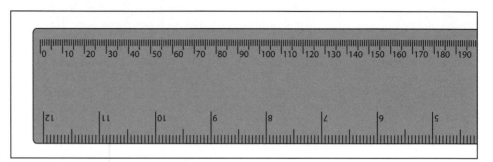

In most styles of music some beats are more significant than others. Like the centimetre marks on your ruler, these more significant beats are usually equally spaced. Just as a metre is divided into 1000 millimetres, every tenth of which is given particular importance by being the start of a new centimetre, so a piece could be 1000 beats long, with, perhaps, every fourth beat given prominence. These important beats are easy to find in musical notation, because they come at the start of each bar. In this imaginary case, the piece would be 250 bars long with four beats in each bar, the first of each bar being given greater emphasis in the music.

The first beat of each bar (called the **downbeat**) is more important than any of the others. From the first downbeat we can count the number of beats until the next downbeat. This will tell us how many beats there are to each bar. Most music will be in two- (duple), three- (triple) or four- (quadruple) time. This means that every bar will have notes that add up to two, three or four beats respectively.

This information is given at the beginning of a score by the **time signature**, something that looks a little like a fraction at the start of the piece.

 The upper number tells us how many beats there are in a bar.

The lower number tells us what note value is being used to represent the beat in the piece.

It is here that the American names for note values can be helpful. Most of the time music uses crotchets as the main beat; the corresponding American name is 'quarter note' and when crotchets are the beat, the lower number in the time signature is 4. If the piece has a quaver beat, or 'eighth note', the lower number will be 8; if the piece has a minim beat (half note) the lower number will be 2, and so on.

On a musical score, each bar is separated from the next one by a vertical line down the stave, called the barline. This enables a musician to read the music fluently, for it is instantly apparent which note coincides with the strong downbeat.

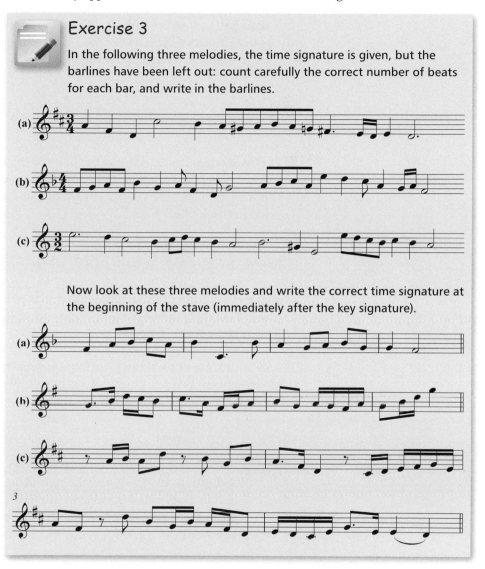

Exercise 3

In the following three melodies, the time signature is given, but the barlines have been left out: count carefully the correct number of beats for each bar, and write in the barlines.

Now look at these three melodies and write the correct time signature at the beginning of the stave (immediately after the key signature).

Metre has a big impact on the character of a piece of music:

- If the metre is in two or four, the music tends to sound direct and purposeful. Most popular music is in this category, as well as music that an army marches in step to: traditionally the left leg leads on the downbeat, and with an even number of beats, and an even number of legs, this will be the same every bar.

March rhythm

- If the metre is in three, the music tends to sound elegant and charming. Many pieces that are based in classical dance forms are in triple time, including the waltz, the sarabande and the menuet. The fact that a bar of three beats naturally tends to subdivide into a 'long half' of two beats and a 'short half' of one beat brings a lilting character to the music. This is mirrored in the actions of, say, a waltz where the leading leg takes more weight than the trailing leg, a very different action to marching.

Waltz rhythm

- If the metre is a more unusual five beats to the bar, the music is likely to sound rather funky, lopsided or tense. Famous examples include the second movement of Tchaikovsky's sixth symphony, Holst's *Mars* from 'The Planets', and Brubeck's *Take Five*.

SIMPLE TIME AND COMPOUND TIME

We began this chapter thinking about a regular pulse or succession of beats, and have seen how these can be organised into bars of (commonly) two, three or four beats to create a sense of metre.

This means that in duple time ($\frac{2}{4}$) each bar is subdivided into two: each subdivision being a crotchet beat. Similarly, in triple time ($\frac{3}{4}$) each bar is subdivided into three, each subdivision again being a crotchet beat.

Top Tips

In music in $\frac{4}{4}$ each bar subdivides into two twice: firstly into half-bars and then beats. This is why the second most significant beat in a bar of four beats is beat 3: the start of the second half of the bar. Neither beats 2 or 4 are as significant; in popular music they are known as the backbeats.

In the same way that each bar can be subdivided this way, so each beat can be subdivided. Indeed, this is usually an essential element to writing successful music: otherwise, the music is likely to lack rhythmic subtlety and the prominence of the beat as a regular, granite-like block tends to become too intrusive and wearing on the ear after a while.

And, just as the bar can comprise subdivisions into two, three or four (or more) beats, so the beat itself can be subdivided into two, three, four, or more.

We have already seen how the character of a piece will be considerably influenced by the composer's choice of metre. In a similar way the decision whether to subdivide the beat into two or three is also important.

Assuming for now that the beat will be represented by crotchets, if this beat is subdivided into two, a pair of quavers is used; if these are in turn subdivided further into two, we have four semiquavers. This creates the most straightforward patterns and the effect could be described as direct and standard.

Music which follows this principle is known as being in **simple time**.

It is also possible, however, to subdivide a beat into three. If this is just the occasional beat that is treated this way in an otherwise simple time context, then we use the notational device of a triplet (see page 17); however, a different approach is used if every beat is divided into three.

Instead of writing triplets the whole time, the main beat is represented by a dotted note, or the value of 1½, which naturally comprises not 2, but 3 notes of the smaller value. So if the note value chosen for the main beat was dotted crotchets, this would comprise 3 quavers; if the main beat was represented by a dotted minim, this would be subdivided into 3 crotchets.

This kind of metre is known as **compound time**.

Compound time is characterised by the beat breaking down into a long-short pattern, which we might call a 'tum-ti-tum' pattern. At a fast tempo, this skips along; at a slower tempo it is elegant and has an appealing lilting quality to the rhythm.

The time signatures in compound music can cause some confusion. We have seen that in simple time the lower number tells us what note value is being treated as the beat (following the American names for the note values). In compound time the main beat will be a dotted note, and there are no equivalent numbers that represent dotted note values. Instead, we use a time signature that counts the smaller note values that are the subdivisions of the main beats (and come in groups of three).

Top Tips

A compound time metre of two dotted crotchets in a bar has the time signature of $\frac{6}{8}$, since each beat comprises a group of three quavers, and quavers are known as 'eighth notes'. The telltale sign to identify compound time signatures, therefore, is that the upper number is divisible by three – i.e. 6, 9, 12, and so on, these giving respectively 2, 3 and 4 beats in the bar. Here is an example:

Compound time

Exercise 4

Look carefully at the following four melodies and work out whether each one is in a simple or compound time. Then count the beats and write the time signature at the beginning of the stave (immediately after the clef):

CHARACTERISTIC RHYTHMIC PATTERNS

There are many recordings of the third Brandenburg concerto available. For example listen to it on the CD: J.S. Bach Brandenburg concertos (Naxos 8.557755).

Rhythm is very important in bringing a particular sense of musical character to a piece. This usually happens when a group of just a few notes has a rhythmic identity that is used many times over. A good example is the opening to Bach's third *Brandenburg* concerto. There is a sense of vigorous energy from the start here, and it is largely due to the recurring group of two semiquavers followed by a quaver:

J. S. Bach: *Brandenburg* concerto No. 3

Listening ideas

You may like to listen to the whole of this movement – this simple little rhythmic 'cell' of just three notes comes again and again: sometimes in the top line (violins), but also in other parts including the bass.

There are some other similar rhythmic flavourings that you will come across:

1. Dotted rhythms

These rhythms are so-called because they use 'dotted' note values (see page 11), followed by shorter notes (e.g. dotted crotchet followed by quaver, or dotted quaver followed by semiquaver). The result is a clipped, quite formal kind of effect that can become quite angry at a brisk tempo. These two melodies by Handel illustrate these two sides of dotted rhythms:

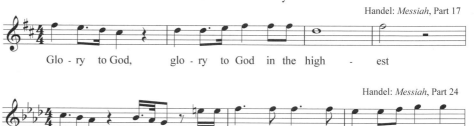

> Note just how often the grouping of dotted quaver and semiquaver comes in these themes.

2. Triplet rhythms

When a single pregnancy produces three babies, they are known as triplets: when a single note value is subdivided into three notes, these too are called triplets. Thus a crotchet can be replaced by three triplet quavers, a minim can be replaced by three triplet crotchets, and so forth. In music notation the three notes of the triplet are bracketed together.

The use of triplets in a simple time metre is always a good effect. There's something fresh-sounding about them, because neither the second nor the third note occurs at a point in the beat that is available through just subdividing into two or four. The triplets in the middle phrase of 'On the Street Where You Live' from the musical My Fair Lady (music by Frederick Loewe) is a good example of triplets in action:

3. Syncopation

Syncopation happens when a note that occurs at a usually unimportant moment in the rhythm becomes stressed, perhaps with an accent. This creates a 'kick' in the rhythm and makes for quite an energetic rhythmic character. Many kinds of jazz and popular music use syncopation, and it is also found in many world music styles, especially those from Africa.

Syncopation can occur in different ways. The simplest is to accent the half beat instead of the main beat as in this melody:

You may have heard, or even have learned to play, Debussy's piano piece *Le Petit Nègre* which has a quicker syncopation that accents the quarter beat:

Debussy: *Le Petit Nègre*

> Note how many times this semiquaver + quaver + semiquaver pattern is used through this short piece, maintaining the character of this quirky music.

Gershwin combines various syncopations to create an appropriately complex rhythmic pattern for his famous song 'I've got rhythm':

Gershwin: *I've Got Rhythm*

half-beat syncopation   quarter beat syncopation   three-quarter beat syncopation   same rhythm as bars 1–2

I_____ got rhy - thm,_____   I_____ got mu - sic,_____

> Notice how this complex rhythm is re-used throughout the song by Gershwin, thereby allowing the listener to grasp the character of this rhythm and trust in its effect being sustained through the song.

 ## Composing ideas

When you are composing your own music think carefully about how to use rhythm to generate musical character in your piece. There are two extremes to be avoided:

- Relying too much on crotchets in forming the beat, perhaps with just the occasional quaver; this can be a very bland and dull effect for your listeners
- Including too many different rhythmic features, each with a strong, but conflicting musical character; this can result in a very confusing and unsettling effect for your listeners.

DEVELOPING RHYTHMIC PATTERNS

It is possible to extend a rhythmic cell just through repeating it and write a lengthy section of music before introducing any new rhythmic material. A famous example of this is the opening to Beethoven's fifth symphony, with its obsessive use of ♩ ♩ ♩ 𝅗𝅥 throughout the texture.

Composing ideas

Think about the energising effect of the short quaver rest in this rhythmic cell: the piece would be wholly less effective if every rest was replaced with another note. Composing is not just about finding the right note: sometimes it is better to use a rest.

Relying on repetition as the main way to develop a rhythmic idea, however, can be a little monotonous. There are other ways to manipulate your rhythmic ideas. Elgar tried reversing a rhythmic cell for his theme in the *Enigma* Variations; see how the rhythm in alternate bars is the same, but in between the pattern is reversed:

Elgar: *Enigma* variations theme

It is also possible to keep all the notes of your rhythmic idea in the same order, but develop the idea by halving or doubling the lenghth of all the notes. Other options are available; for instance, in triple time, each note could be trebled in length. This way they keep the same ratio, but become more, or less, energised.

When the note values are increased (perhaps doubled), the technique is called **augmentation**.

When the note values are reduced (perhaps halved), the technique is called **diminution**.

Exercise 5

The following melody illustrates the process being used in both directions; the rhythmic pattern of the first two bars is used for the remainder of the phrase. Can you identity all the uses of augmentation and diminution?

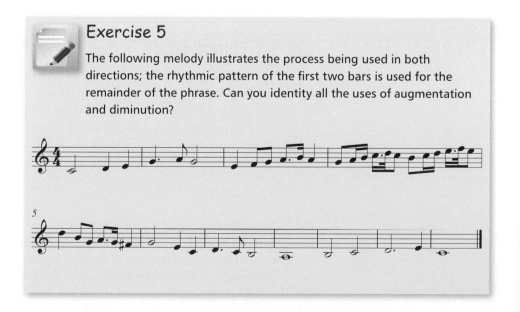

Some styles of music make use of an opportunity to reorganise the natural pattern of the metre.

One such example is regularly found in Latin American musical styles such as the **rumba**. Most rumbas are notated in $\frac{4}{4}$ time, but it is quite hard to hear the four beats, or even the crotchet pulse when the music is played. This is because the style reorganises the eight quavers that are available in $\frac{4}{4}$ metre.

Most music in $\frac{4}{4}$ time emphasises the first, third, fifth and seventh quavers more than the second, fourth, sixth and eighth quavers. This highlights the four beats in each bar and makes a lot of music in $\frac{4}{4}$ time suitable for marching to.

In many Latin styles, the quavers that are emphasised are the first, fourth and seventh ones. This leads to a rather infectious rhythmic character that seems to have three beats in the bar: two of them being dotted crotchets (as in compound time) and the final one a normal crotchet (as in simple time). This asymmetric organisation of the half-beats in the bar cuts across the normal four crotchet beats we expect in $\frac{4}{4}$ and the result is called a **cross-rhythm**.

Here is the comparison:

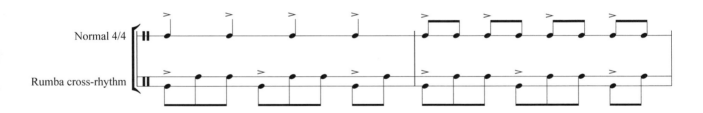

Normal 4/4

Rumba cross-rhythm

Things to do

Try tapping out the rumba rhythm: use your left hand for the notes on the lower line and your right hand for notes on the upper line; there should be a regular series of taps in the following order: L R R L R R L R. Then repeat. As you get used to the pattern, accent the left hand more than the right: you should get the sense of three beats in the bar: two long ones followed by a short one.

There is a particular cross-rhythm that occurs sometimes in music in triple time. This is called a **hemiola**. In triple time the emphasised beat usually comes every third beat and is on the downbeat of the bar. In a hemiola two bars are treated rather differently, with alternate beats emphasised. You might think this should sound a quicker rhythm, but in fact it can feel half-speed as though each beat were twice as long. This is because you have to go two bars before the first beat of the bar is again emphasised:

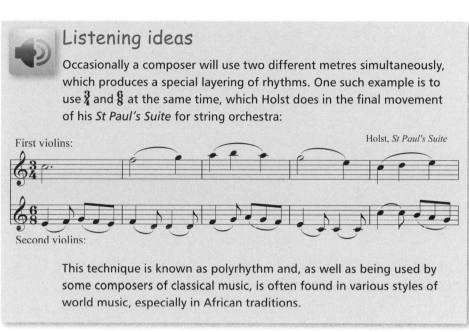

Listening ideas

Occasionally a composer will use two different metres simultaneously, which produces a special layering of rhythms. One such example is to use ¾ and ⁶⁄₈ at the same time, which Holst does in the final movement of his *St Paul's Suite* for string orchestra:

Holst, *St Paul's Suite*

This technique is known as polyrhythm and, as well as being used by some composers of classical music, is often found in various styles of world music, especially in African traditions.

LESS STRICT RHYTHMS

Most music has a strict pulse, but there are some exceptions to this. Among these are:

1. **Irregular metres**: sometimes, especially in more recent styles of 20th-century classical music, the composer changes the time signature frequently which prevents a sense of regularity from getting established.

2. **Free time**: in some music the sense of rhythm is deliberately rather vague and left to the performer's discretion. This will include vocal music where singers are encouraged to recite a lot of words to a natural speech rhythm, and solo passages such as cadenzas in instrumental pieces.

3. **Rubato**: this term, meaning 'robbed time', is used to describe accurately notated rhythms that are played with a degree of approximation in order to bring out the expressive quality of the music; it is, therefore, often used by performers when playing Romantic music. Jazz singers often use a similar skill when they sing the melody of some standards with particular freedom, often anticipating the beat, while their accompanying band maintains a strict pulse and metre.

Exercise 6

Test yourself on the special vocabulary concerning Area of Study 1 – Rhythm and Metre. Which terms are being described here?

a. An accent on a note that does not occur on the beat
b. A note that is three crotchet beats long
c. A rhythm which is repeated but with every note halved in value
d. Music in which the main beat is always subdivided into three
e. Music in which a single beat is subdivided into three
f. A metre with four beats: beats 1–3 are each a crotchet, but the fourth beat is a dotted crotchet
g. An expressive performance style in which the rhythm is played slightly approximately
h. Music in which two metres are used simultaneously.

MELODY

INTRODUCING PITCH

A small amount of music exists without the need for real pitch, in other words tuned notes that you can sing back accurately in tune. Such pitch-less music includes solos written for drum-kit and various styles of drumming found in world music, relying on rhythm, timbre, texture and dynamic for its effect.

As fascinating and exciting as this kind of music can be, before long it can seem rather restricted unless one introduces the element of pitch. Pitch enables us to enjoy melodies that we can sing, and harmonies that can bring so much colour and richness to music. Pitch also makes available the vast array of timbres of tuned instruments from around the world.

Top Tips

If you have been learning to play a tuned instrument for a while, you will probably be experienced in reading pitch to some extent. If this is still unfamiliar to you as you start your GCSE course, it should be a priority to learn this now.

The standard system for notating pitch has been evolving since medieval days. The most fundamental element is the octave. An octave comprises two notes that are clearly high and low, but which sound very similar in pitch; the reason for this is at the heart of the physics of sound. The octave is – as the name implies – essentially broken into eight. The first seven notes are given letter names –

A to G – and the eighth note, sounding so much like the first note, is also given the letter 'A', whereupon the pattern starts all over again.

These seven notes – A to G – are shown on a series of lines and spaces. With seven notes in the recurring pattern a note that is on a line in one octave – for instance, 'middle' C – will be in a space in the octaves either side – 'tenor' C and 'treble' C. In theory, these lines and spaces carry on for ever in both directions (or at least for the spectrum of pitch audible to the human ear) but printing all these would look crazy and be very hard to read from, so the convention is that musicians rely on just five lines for the stave. A sign, known as the **clef**, at the start of each stave identifies which five lines are being used. When an extra line is required for a particular note, a short section of the next line is used just where that note appears (this is known as a leger line).

The two most common clefs are the treble and bass clefs which work as follows:

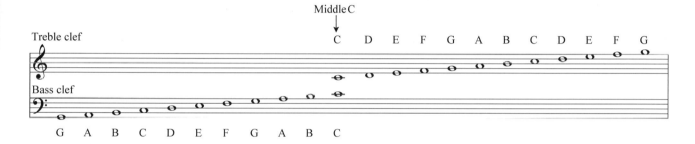

You should aim to be fluent in reading the notes in these two clefs as soon as you can: this will make many parts of the course much more straightforward for you and make much more music accessible to you.

The seven pitches A to G cover all the white keys on a piano (over seven octaves).

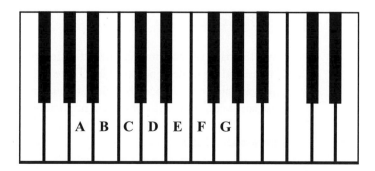

You will be aware, however, that there are a further five black keys. These five notes are described as being sharps (♯) or flats (♭). Each can be described in two ways:

- ◼ Starting at C, move to play the black note to the right which will raise the pitch. This is C♯.
- ◼ Starting at D, move to play the black note to the left which will lower the pitch. This is D♭.
- ◼ However, the actual key you are playing in these two descriptions is the same one.

Where there is no black note between two white keys on the piano – between E and F, and between B and C – there is a slightly different overlap. E flat is the black note to the left of E; there is no black note to the right between E and F, so E sharp is actually an alternative name for F. Similarly, F flat is another name for E.

It is very important to understand that the gap between a note and its immediate neighbour on the keyboard is called a **semitone**.

Examples of semitones include:

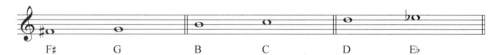

| F♯ | G | | B | C | | D | E♭ |

Similarly the gap between a note and the next-but-one neighbouring note is called a **tone**. Examples of tones include:

| D | E | | F♯ | G♯ | | B♭ | C |

> In practice, these more complicated flats and sharps are quite unusual and not likely to bother you much at GCSE.

TYPES OF SCALE

Scales are the basis of most music. The definition of a scale is: a group of notes played in ascending or descending order. There are an almost infinite number of patterns available on a piano keyboard that you can devise that fulfil that definition. There are some common ones which are important for you to know at GCSE:

1. **Pentatonic Scales**:

   You may have come across the word 'pentagon', which is a five-sided shape in geometry. In the USA, their military headquarters is a huge building with five sides, so reporters often talk about 'The Pentagon' in their reports.

You may, therefore, quickly realise that a pentatonic scale uses only five notes. The most obvious pentatonic scale is the one using all the black notes on the piano and no white notes. This is notated thus:

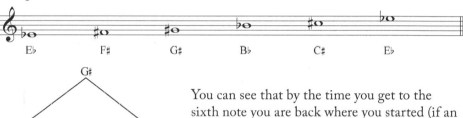

Eb   F#   G#   Bb   C#   Eb

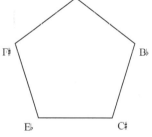

You can see that by the time you get to the sixth note you are back where you started (if an octave higher). It is rather like going round this pentagon-based diagram:

This particular pentatonic scale is very significant, because there are no semi-tone gaps involved: every note is a tone or more away from the next notes in the scale. This can create something of an oriental, or Chinese, flavour to the music.

Sometimes composers use pentatonic scales that do involve a semitone, such as this scale that uses some of the 'white' notes:

D   E   F   A   B   D

However, such scales are less typical of pentatonic music, and do not have such a strong exotic flavour.

2. Chromatic scale

'Chroma' is the Greek word meaning 'colour', and the chromatic scale is the one using all 12 notes of a piano keyboard – with all these notes available, a composer can make any musical 'colour' in their work. You might think of the chromatic scale as music's equivalent to a comprehensive colour chart. Here is the notation for a chromatic scale:

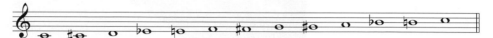

Music that makes heavy use of chromatic scales can sound very opulent and complex, rather like a meal with very rich foods for every course.

3. Whole tone scale

The whole tone scale is exactly what it says in the name: a scale where every step from one note to the next is a whole tone (i.e. not a semitone). This creates a scale of six different pitches. There are two different collections of notes that are whole tone scales, depending on whether you start on C or C#:

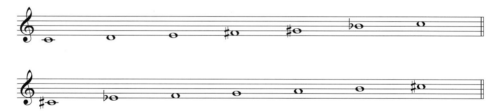

Music based on whole tone scales tends to sound rather airy and wispy. This is because it is difficult to sense any kind of key note.

Here is the opening to a piano piece by Debussy that is based on a whole tone scale. It is called 'Voiles', which means 'Sails' (or perhaps 'Veils'): the music paints a picture of them being caught in the wind.

Debussy: *Voiles*

4. Diatonic scales

Diatonic scales are of central importance to the vast majority of music that the western world has generated over the past thousand years. There are several varieties, but they all share a similar definition: a seven-note scale which has five tones and two semitones to arrive at the note an octave higher than where it started.

The two semitones can be used at various stages of the scale. The most familiar pattern is what we call the **major scale**. This is the pattern you will hear if you play the white notes on the piano starting at C and going stepwise upwards to the next C. It is easy to see that between the third and the fourth notes (E–F) and the seventh and eighth (B–C) there is no black note: these are, therefore, the places where the semitones are used in a major scale.

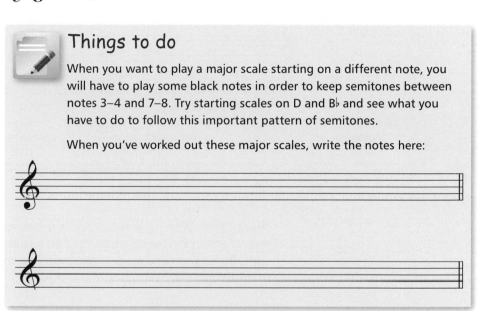

Things to do

When you want to play a major scale starting on a different note, you will have to play some black notes in order to keep semitones between notes 3–4 and 7–8. Try starting scales on D and B♭ and see what you have to do to follow this important pattern of semitones.

When you've worked out these major scales, write the notes here:

A second important pattern for a diatonic scale is the pattern we call the **minor scale**. This is the pattern you will hear if you play the white notes on the piano starting at A and going stepwise downwards to the next A. Now try going back upwards: it is easy to see that between the second and the third notes (B–C) and the fifth and sixth (E–F) there is no black note: these are, therefore, the places where the semitones are used in a major scale.

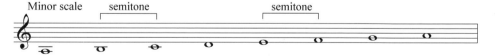

Minor scales tend to be rather more complex than their major counterparts. Playing the scale above in a downwards direction should sound convincing to you, but what about going upwards: are the last few notes satisfactory? Try using a G♯: does that improve the effect? Now try F♯ and G♯: which is the best option?

In all there are three versions of the minor scale, giving us options over the sixth and seventh degrees of the scale. It is a good idea to learn the names and definitions for these:

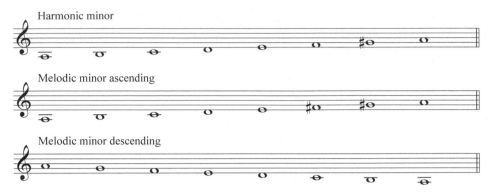

Sometimes it is useful to remember all three patterns when you are writing a tune in a minor key:

Music based on major or minor scales is known as **tonal** music. There are several other patterns for where the two semitones can appear in a diatonic scale. These are called **modes**. There are four traditional modes that date back to medieval days.

These were also used by a wide range of musicians in the 20th century, from classical composers like Vaughan Williams, to pop groups such as the Beatles. Music based on these modes is known as **modal** music.

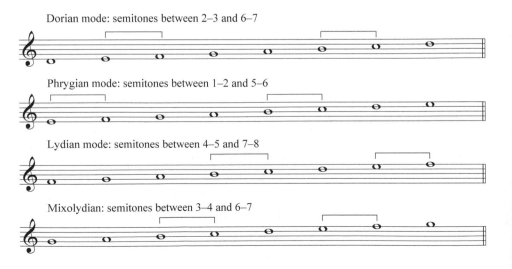

Each mode has a different musical character. The higher up the scale the two semitones occur, the brighter the resultant scale and music will sound; conversely, the lower they occur in the scale, the darker and gloomier the resulting scale and music will sound. The following chart shows how this works out:

	1–2	2–3	3–4	4–5	5–6	6–7	7–8
Lydian mode				*			*
Major scale			*				*
Mixolydian mode			*			*	
Dorian mode		*				*	
Melodic minor (descending)		*			*		
Phrygian mode	*				*		

⋆ = where semitones occur

Top Tips

For GCSE you will not need to known the different modes by name and definition, but you may need to be able to tell the difference between the three 'M's: Major, Minor and Modal.

Music written using these modes will not sound so different from tonal music: there are still eight notes to the octave, with a sense of keynote or tonic. The chart above suggests that music in the lydian mode will sound a little brighter than music in a major key, while music in the mixolydian mode will sound a little less bright than major key music. Similarly, music in the phrygian mode will sound darker than music in a minor key, while music in the dorian mode will sound a little less dark than minor key music.

Exercise 7

To test your understanding of scales, complete each of the following scales as they are described on the previous pages. Remember to write sharps and flats in front of the notes requiring them.

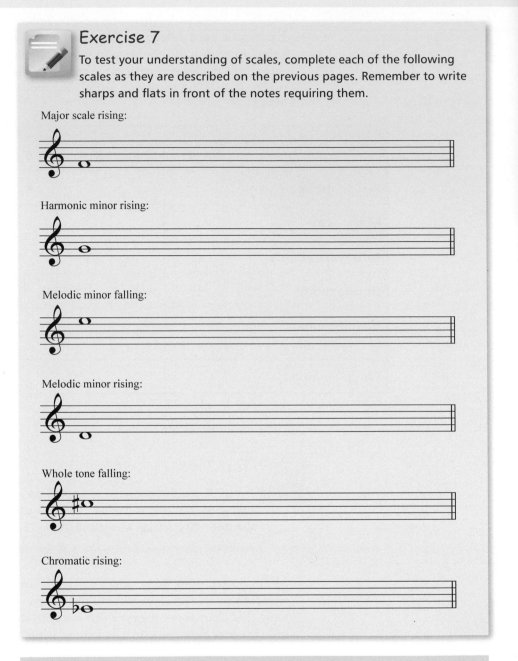

Major scale rising:

Harmonic minor rising:

Melodic minor falling:

Melodic minor rising:

Whole tone falling:

Chromatic rising:

INTERVALS

'Interval' is the gap between two notes. The two notes can be:

- Played simultaneously in a chord (appearing vertically in the music): this makes for a harmonic interval
- Played successively in a melody (appearing horizontally in the music): this makes for a melodic interval.

It is important to be able to measure the gap in pitch between these two notes. The system for doing this uses two components: an adjective and a number.

To work out the number, count the lower note as one and then count up the relevant letters (A–G) until you reach the upper note. The number you reach is the 'size' of the interval:

This only takes us so far though: both D to F and D to F♯ are 3rds, but they sound different. This is where the adjective comes in: it helps to define the quality of the interval.

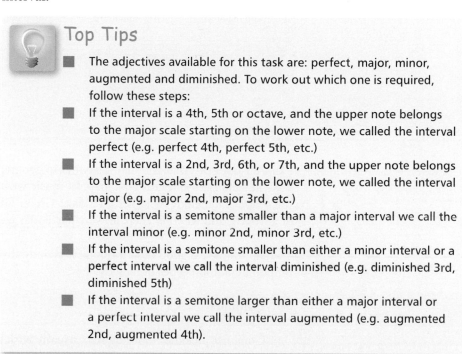

Top Tips

- The adjectives available for this task are: perfect, major, minor, augmented and diminished. To work out which one is required, follow these steps:
- If the interval is a 4th, 5th or octave, and the upper note belongs to the major scale starting on the lower note, we called the interval perfect (e.g. perfect 4th, perfect 5th, etc.)
- If the interval is a 2nd, 3rd, 6th, or 7th, and the upper note belongs to the major scale starting on the lower note, we called the interval major (e.g. major 2nd, major 3rd, etc.)
- If the interval is a semitone smaller than a major interval we call the interval minor (e.g. minor 2nd, minor 3rd, etc.)
- If the interval is a semitone smaller than either a minor interval or a perfect interval we call the interval diminished (e.g. diminished 3rd, diminished 5th)
- If the interval is a semitone larger than either a major interval or a perfect interval we call the interval augmented (e.g. augmented 2nd, augmented 4th).

Here is a range of intervals and the correct definition for each one. Make sure you understand why each example is called as it is:

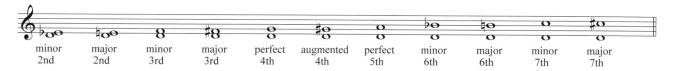

Exercise 8

Analyse each of the following intervals. Remember to give a number and an adjective, and to start counting with the lower note as '1':

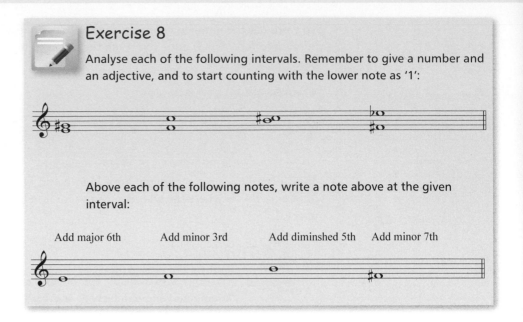

Above each of the following notes, write a note above at the given interval:

Add major 6th   Add minor 3rd   Add diminshed 5th   Add minor 7th

CONTOURS

Contour is a word that you may have met in geography; it is a way of charting the way the land rises and falls on a map. In music we use the same word to describe the shape of a melody: whether it tends to rise or fall, whether it does so gradually or abruptly, and whether there are any particular patterns used in the tune.

To help us make a good description of a melody there are certain words which pinpoint common types of melody:

1. Conjunct

Conjunct melodies move by step, usually with a mix of upwards and downwards movements. This should be easy to spot on the page, and with a little training you should be able to hear that a melody is conjunct: the effect is usually very smooth and easy to sing, even when the music is fast.

Conjunct melody

2. Scalic

As the name implies, this word describes a melodic line that is built from scale patterns. This means it is a particular type of conjunct melody. The opening of Vivaldi's violin concerto in A minor, Op. 3 No. 8, could be described this way:

Scalic melody

3. Disjunct

Choosing the right word is a matter of balance: a melody that involves an occasional small leap but is otherwise stepwise will still be called conjunct (e.g. the opening of Rachmaninov's third piano concerto).

Similarly, a melody with a lot of leaps, but including a few stepwise moves will still be called disjunct (e.g. the opening of Shostakovich's fifth symphony).

Disjunct means the opposite of conjunct, and describes a melodic line full of leaps. This should be easy to spot on the page and by ear: the effect is usually rather bold and energetic; disjunct melodies are often tricky to sing.

Disjunct melody

4. Triadic

We shall meet triads in the harmony section of this chapter. They are three-note chords, which can be arranged so that the middle note is a 3rd above the lowest note, and the top note is a 3rd above the middle note. When this group of three notes is played simultaneously (notes vertical on the page) one hears a chord; when the notes are played successively (notes horizontal on the page), repeating as the composer sees fit, we hear a melodic line that can be described as being triadic. A good example is the opening of Mozart's *Eine kleine Nachtmusik*:

All notes of G major chord   All notes of D7 chord

You can see that there are no stepwise moves here, so the melody can also be considered to be disjunct, but the actual notes used make a G major chord (G – up a 3rd to B – up another 3rd to D) means that this is a triadic melodic phrase.

5. Arpeggio

An arpeggio is a particular kind of triadic contour in which the melody takes the three notes of a triad and, instead of mixing them up, plays them in rising or descending order. A famous example comes in Prokofiev's ballet *Romeo and Juliet*:

E minor arpeggio   B minor arpeggio

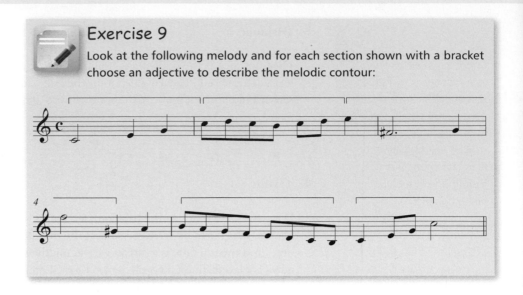

Exercise 9

Look at the following melody and for each section shown with a bracket choose an adjective to describe the melodic contour:

SPECIAL MELODIC NOTES

Looking at melodic contour requires us to look with some breadth at the direction of a melody or phrase. It is also necessary to spot some specific details.

1. **Passing note**

   Passing notes quite simply enable the melody to 'pass' from one significant note to the next in a conjunct, or stepwise, fashion. The notes either side of the passing note fit the accompanying chord well, but the passing note wouldn't if emphasised; however, although this is not always the case, you can expect passing notes to be off the beat, and this, coupled with the natural flow of the conjunct motion, means you are barely aware of the clash between the passing note and the accompanying chord.

   The effect of passing notes, therefore, is to smooth out what would otherwise be a very disjunct (and probably triadic) melodic contour. The opening theme from Bach's second *Brandenburg* concerto would be relentlessly triadic and rhythmically monotonous without its four B♭s, each of which is a passing note and helps to create a much more memorable melody:

J. S. Bach, *Brandenburg* concerto No. 2

2. **Appoggiatura**

   An appoggiatura is a particularly expressive note in a melodic phrase. Approached by a leap it is a dissonant note, usually heard on a strong beat, that resolves to a consonant note by step a beat later.

For definition of the terms 'consonant' and 'dissonant', see page 46.

It is more common for an appoggiatura to resolve downwards, but they can resolve upwards. Appoggiaturas can also be chromatic notes, for extra expressive intensity.

appoggiaturas

chromatic
appoggiatura

3. Blue notes

Blue notes are particular notes found in jazz styles, above all the **blues**. Typically, these are flattened version of the 3rd, 5th and 7th degrees of the scale, giving a rather sour, dark and minor colour to the melody when the harmony is essentially major.

All three of the standard blue notes occur in this phrase:

Exercise 10

Play through the following melody and find examples of a passing note, an appoggiatura and a blue note:

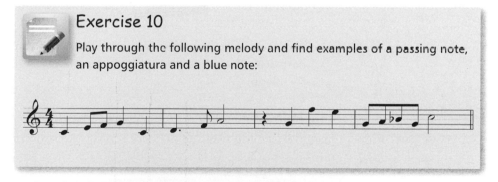

DECORATING MELODIES

In some styles of music the melody is often decorated using a variety of special effects.

In music of the Baroque period (c. 1600–1750) composers often expected the melodic line to be decorated with trills and mordents.

Mordents bring a sense of attack to the start of a note, by playing the note itself, a note one step above, and then the original note again in very quick succession.

If the second note is a step below the main note, this is called an **inverted mordent**.

The effect is to draw attention to specific notes, no more so than at the start of Bach's famous Toccata in D minor for organ which begins with an inverted mordent.

J. S. Bach: Toccata in D minor

The device was very effective on keyboard instruments such as the organ and harpsichord which do not play louder when you press harder (as happens on the piano).

Trills are a somewhat more prolonged ornament in which the main note alternates rapidly with the note above.

In the Classical period (c. 1740–1820) composers continued to use the **trill**, often at perfect cadences most notably at the end of a cadenza in a concerto. A typical example is this cadence from Mozart's piano sonata in B♭, K. 333, first movement:

Mozart, Piano sonata in B♭ K. 333

A new ornament became popular in the Classical period: the **turn**. This tends to appear in slower pieces and decorates a melodic note with a four-note formula:

- The note above the written note
- The written note
- The note below the written note
- The written note.

The effect is a very elegant and graceful melodic shape that typifies the Classical style. The theme from Mozart's piano sonata in F, K. 332, second movement illustrates this well:

Mozart: Piano sonata in F, K. 332, second movement

In the Romantic period (c. 1810–1920) the **appoggiatura** became the favoured way to enhance a melodic line. Not only did appoggiaturas become more frequent, they also tended to become longer too, since this helped to heighten the emotional pull of the music, which was greatly appealing to the sensibilities of the day. Composers such as Schumann (1810–1856) and Mahler (1860–1911) explored this in much of their music.

In the Modern era (since 1910) composers have favoured decoration of greater impact. Some of the influence for this has come in popular styles, such as jazz.

The **acciaccatura** (or 'grace note') accents a note by preceding it with a very short, split second of a neighbouring note which is written at a smaller size with a line through its tail:

Composers sometimes write glissandos on the piano, but in reality this is usually just a very fast C major or chromatic scale rather than real consistent sliding of the pitch.

Jazz and other popular styles have also given rise to effects that use a slide in the pitch of a note. Most wind and string instruments can create this sliding effect which is not possible in the same way on the piano where there is no way of bridging the gap in pitch between each note.

A **glissando** calls for a slide between two notes (the French word 'glisser' means 'to slide'). The famous opening of Gershwin's *Rhapsody in Blue* includes a thrilling glissando for solo clarinet.

Less dramatic, but of a similar principle are notes which are played with some deliberate changing of the pitch in a technique called **pitch bending**. This is done in many modern styles and on instruments ranging from brass and saxophones to bass guitars and singers.

Exercise 11

Where might you expect to find long trills in a Classical period concerto?

Why did Baroque composers use the inverted mordent on some notes?

What is the difference between an acciaccatura and a mordent?

Which period used the turn as a form of melodic decoration?

Why is a true glissando not possible on the piano?

DEVELOPING MELODIES

Some melodies seem to grow in a natural, free-flowing way. Sometimes, however, they develop with various techniques consciously deployed by the composer.

The simplest method is to repeat a particular short melodic shape. When this happens the result is often an **ostinato**: a repeating figure that carries on with a sense of propulsion while other layers in the texture change and provide interest. The modern style called **Minimalism** is largely built on this technique.

Often in pop and rock styles a melodic pattern in the bass is repeated as an underpinning to the song. This is known as a **riff**.

A **sequence** is a related idea. A short phrase or shape in the melody is repeated, but the pitch is changed: every note is moved up or down by a number of steps. The following melody uses two sequences:

Falling sequence of previous two bars (down a 5th)

Occasionally a melody can be developed by being turned upside down, leading to a version of the tune called an **inversion**. In this technique, the intervals stay the same size, but everyone is taken in the opposite direction: what originally went upwards now goes downwards, and vice versa.

Inversion of previous two bars

MELODIC PHRASING

Once a melody has been composed, decorated and developed, there remains one further aspect which can bring character to the music. This is the phrasing and articulation.

There are a few terms and symbols with which you need to be familiar:

Term	Symbol	Definition
Legato	⌒	Very smooth playing with all notes joined up evenly
Staccato	.	Detached playing with each note quickly released to create gap before the next note
Staccatissimo	▾	A more extreme version of staccato; very short notes
Marcato	–	Notes are joined up, but the start of each note is 'marked' – given extra attack – which reduces the smooth effect
Accent	>	A strong attack to emphasise a particular note

Try playing the following melody, taking particular care to observe all the phrasing and articulation instructions:

You might like to compose your own melodies that use the full range of phrasing marks.

Some aspects of phrasing are dependent on the specific choice of instrument being used to play the music. Wind players have to breathe, string players have to change the direction the bow is moving, and so on. More information on these aspects can be found on pages 53–56.

© www.shutterstock.com

TONALITY

KEYS

We have already considered the difference between the various types of diatonic scale (see page 27). The fundamental difference here is between **tonality** (major and minor scales) and **modality** (dorian, phrygian, lydian and mixolydian scales).

It is probable that the majority of music you have heard is tonal music. When it comes to matters of harmony, it is important to understand the tonal system a little further.

On page 27 we saw how a major scale starting on C uses only 'white' notes on the piano (no sharps or flats) and this gives a scale with semitones between degrees 3–4 and 7–8.

If we begin on G – a perfect 5th above C – and keep semitones in the same place, it will be necessary to introduce F♯ into the scale. Music in G major is therefore written with one sharp (F♯) in the key signature at the start of the piece (and duplicated on every stave).

If we begin on F – a perfect 5th below C – and keep semitones in the same place, it will be necessary to introduce B♭ into the scale. Music in F major is therefore written with one flat (B♭) in the key signature at the start of the piece (and duplicated on every stave).

So, starting on C there is no sharp or flat in the key signature. Starting a 5th higher there is one sharp; starting a 5th lower there is one flat. A pattern is emerging: if we start another 5th higher – not on G, but D – we will require two sharps (F♯ and C♯); for a scale starting another 5th lower – not on F, but on B♭ – it will be necessary to have two flats (B♭ and E♭).

If you extend this pattern further, you reach a point after six steps in one direction that a scale starting on F♯ requires six sharps; meanwhile a scale starting on G♭ requires six flats. At this point you may look at your piano keyboard and conclude that F♯ and G♭ are essentially the same note, and that you have come full circle. This enables you to devise the following diagram of key signatures:

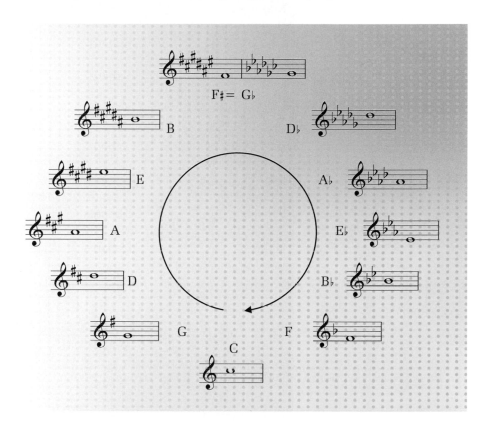

This diagram is known as the circle of 5ths and is of considerable significance in tonal music.

Major keys are only one half of the tonal system; it is also important to understand how minor keys relate to the system of key signatures.

Earlier on page 28 we found that going downwards on the white keys from A to A produces a convincing minor scale without using any 'black' notes (sharps or flats). We also found that in some forms it is attractive to sharpen the 6th and 7th degrees of the minor scale, especially when going up the scale. Despite this, it is the descending form that defines the key signature of minor keys.

Therefore the keys of C major and A minor share the same key signature (requiring no flats or sharps), and are described as 'relative' keys:

- A minor is the **relative minor** of C major
- C major is the **relative major** or A minor.

A is three semitones (or a minor 3rd) lower than C; the same relationship between relative major and relative minor will exist throughout the tonal system. The following table can be deduced:

Major key	Key Signature	Minor key
C major	0 sharps	A minor
G major	1 sharp	E minor
D major	2 sharps	B minor
A major	3 sharps	F♯ minor
E major	4 sharps	C♯ minor
B major	5 sharps	G♯ minor
F♯ major	6 sharps	D♯ minor
G♭ major	6 flats	E♭ minor
D♭ major	5 flats	B♭ minor
A♭ major	4 flats	F minor
E♭ major	3 flats	C minor
B♭ major	2 flats	G minor
F major	1 flat	D minor
C major	0 flats	A minor

Within the tonal system, each degree of the scale is given a different name that applies whatever key one is using. These are as follows:

1	2	3	4	5	6	7	8
Tonic	Supertonic	Mediant	Subdominant	Dominant	Submediant	Leading note	Tonic

At GCSE you need to make sure you are familiar with the keys that use up to four sharps or flats.

What does it mean to be in a key? Essentially it means that the 12 different pitches available have different degrees of significance.

Most important, by far, is the key note or tonic. Second most important is the 5th degree of the scale or dominant. Next, the mediant and the leading note are important as they provide the major 3rd in the tonic and dominant chords; the leading note, as the name implies, is also significant in leading to the tonic. The subdominant also plays a significant role, since the chord built on this degree of the scale is important. The remaining notes of the diatonic scale – the supertonic and submediant – follow, being more important than the five pitches that do not belong to the scale, but even these play specific roles in relation to the key. For example, in C major, F♯ can be used to emphasise the important dominant note of G.

Exercise 12

Test yourself on tonality and keys with these 10 questions:

1. Which major key requires a key signature of three flats?
2. Which minor key requires a key signature of two sharps?
3. What is the relative minor of A major?
4. What is the relative major of G minor?
5. What note is the dominant of E major?
6. What note is the mediant of C minor?
7. Which major key has B♭ as its subdominant?
8. Which minor key has D♯ as its supertonic?
9. Which notes are not sharps in E major?
10. Which notes are not flats in F minor?

CHANGING KEY

The sense of being in a particular key in tonal music is so strong that considerable effect can be achieved through changing key.

An example of this is Stevie Wonder's song 'I Just Called To Say I Love You'.

In modern popular styles of music, including music theatre, a common technique is moving to a different key for a final chorus, usually a semitone or tone higher. This requires little preparation: the previous section will end in the main key of the song and the new chorus will start in a new key. Factors such as the timing of the change (clearly for a final repeat of the chorus) and the sense of climax supported by the instrumentation and dynamics at this point are usually enough to make the abrupt change convincing.

Sometimes a little extra easing of the change of key is desired: this is usually done by inserting the dominant 7th chord (see page 48) of the new key immediately before the change of key.

This is easy to do, because the original key note (tonic) is also the 3rd of this significant chord:

Many pieces of tonal music use key changes in a more subtle way. This alternative, and more traditional, method differs from the 'last chorus up a key' idea because:

- ■ The change(s) of key will happen during the piece and the music will return to the original key by the end
- ■ The keys used for the change are likely to be much more closely related to the original key.

This kind of changing of key is known as **modulation**.

Take a look at the circle of 5ths diagram of keys (page 41). If a song that starts in A major goes up to B♭ major for its final key signature you can see that the key has moved five steps around the circle: almost to the opposite side.

It is also quite common to modulate to the relative minor; this can include the relative minor of the dominant and subdominant keys too.

In traditional modulation, the keys visited are much more closely connected, usually just a single step one way or the other around the circle, most commonly to the dominant key which, you can see, is one degree sharper (having either one more sharp, or one fewer flat in its key signature).

Therefore, if you want to modulate from G major, which has just one sharp (F♯), to its neighbour in the circle of D major, which has two sharps (F♯ and C♯), it is necessary to change C natural for C♯ at some point.

There are two stages to look out for in a standard modulation (or to include in your composition if you want to use this technique):

For more on cadences, see page 48.

- ■ An initial hint of the new key, using the new accidental (in our example, C♯)
- ■ A cadence in the new key to complete the modulation.

Haydn: Sonata in G major Hob.XVI/8, second movement

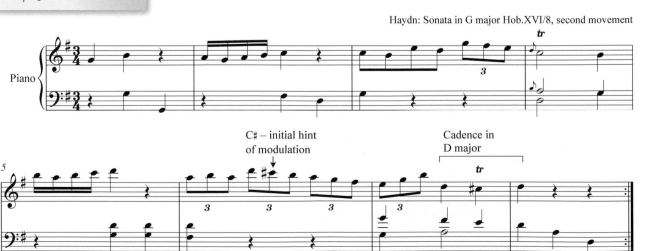

Both these stages are present in the first half of this Menuet by Haydn:

Often the first step is present and not the second. When this happens we usually say there is an inflection (or hint) of another key, but not a full modulation.

In the second half of Haydn's Menuet there is a G♯ in the first bar which might suggest we are in for another modulation, this time to A minor; however, there is never really a full cadence in A minor, so this is just an inflection. Meanwhile, though, Haydn reintroduces a C♮ into the music to propel the music back to G major; the cadence in the fourth bar of this half completes this modulation back to the original key.

Return of C natural
the hint that we're
heading back to
G major

Cadence in G major

Piano

Hint of possible
modulation to
A minor

Exercise 13

Write a second phrase to this opening one which modulates the piece to its dominant key:

Remember to include hint of new key

Cadence in the dominant

HARMONY

CONSONANCE AND DISSONANCE

Harmony is created when two or more different pitches are played simultaneously. Simple experimentation should reveal to you that some combinations of notes sound well together, creating a rich, sonorous effect; others sound less well together, creating a harsh, abrasive sound.

When notes sound well together, they are considered to be **consonant.**

When notes sound clashing, they are considered to be **dissonant.**

Using just a pair of notes, the intervals of a 3rd, 5th, 6th and the octave create **consonance**; the intervals of a 2nd, 4th and 7th create **dissonance**.

It is more common to have three notes in a chord. If you choose to have, in ascending order, C, E and G, the result is very consonant. The E is a 3rd above C, the G is a 3rd above E and also a 5th above C. This is a **root position** chord.

When the order of these notes ascending is E, G and C (on top), the G is still a 3rd above E; the C is now a 6th above E, however the C is also a 4th above G. This is called a **first inversion** chord and is slightly less confident and stable.

When the order is further changed to be G, C and E, although the sound is still attractive with a 6th between G and E and a 3rd between C and E, the 4th between the G at the bottom of the chord and the C above it makes this a more precarious version of the chord. This is called a **second inversion** chord.

Chords using only dissonant intervals sound harsher on the ear, e.g. D, G, C.

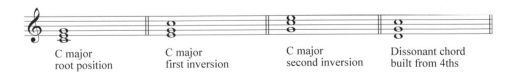

C major   C major   C major   Dissonant chord
root position   first inversion second inversion built from 4ths

© www.educationphotos.co.uk

DIATONIC CHORDS

If the three notes in a chord are separated by two intervals of a 3rd, as in the C, E, G chord on the previous page, then it is called a **triad**.

Triads can be built on any degree of the diatonic scale, in either a major or minor key. This is easily done in written form: if the starting note is on a line, the other two notes should be written on the next two lines; if it is in a space, they should be written in the next two spaces.

Remember that the key signature may affect the notes of each chord. This will affect whether each chord will be a major or minor chord, or perhaps neither. The way these work out is the same for every major key, because the pattern of tones and semitones is the same for every major scale.

The resulting chords can be referred to either by letter name (in a method used by guitarists), or according to the degree of the scale using Roman numerals (capital for major chords; lower case for minor chords).

Here are the triads for each note of a C major scale:

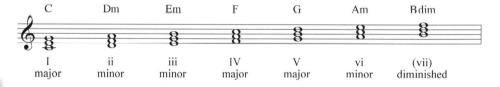

Notice here that the scale formed by the lowest notes (roots) of these chords, and the scale formed by the middle note (the 3rds) of the chords, are harmonic minor scales.

The situation regarding triads and harmony in a minor key is more complicated due to the various options for the 6th and 7th degrees of the scale which can be sharpened should you wish (see page 28). Here is one common way they can be worked out, in this instance in D minor:

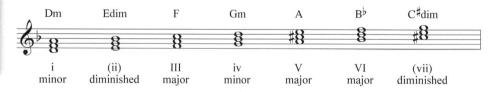

Accidentals can appear in the harmony at times. Sometimes this is because the music is in a minor key, and sometimes because it is modulating; at other times, particularly if there are no accidentals in the melody, this is just to bring extra colour to the music, and is called **chromatic harmony**.

In both major and minor keys, the dominant chord is usually major (in the minor key this requires using an accidental for the 3rd degree of the chord). So in both C major and C minor, the dominant chord will be that of G major.

The dominant chord is also likely to have an extra note. Like all other triads, it already has a root, 3rd and 5th; with the dominant it is common to extend this pattern further and add a 7th (i.e. two notes above the 5th). We call this the chord of the dominant 7th, and it is always likely to move onto the tonic chord. There are various shorthand notations for this chord as follows:

CADENCES

Cadences are a musical equivalent to punctuation in prose. Like punctuation, they occur at the end of a phrase, and they comprise a pattern of two chords. There are four types in all, falling into two categories:

- Cadences that end on chord I: **perfect cadence, plagal cadence**
- Cadences that do not end on chord I: **interrupted cadence, imperfect cadence**.

In the first category, when the phrase stops on the tonic chord it will sound like the piece could be finished; this is rather like a full stop. In the second category, because the phrase finished on some other chord, it will sound like the piece cannot possibly be finished; this is rather like having just a comma or a colon.

The definition of each type of cadence is as follows:

1. **Perfect cadence**
   The chord progression in a perfect cadence is from the dominant to the tonic (V to I), which sounds very confident and conclusive:

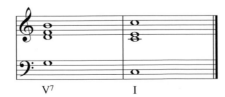

2. Plagal cadence

The plagal cadence has the subdominant chord leading to the tonic (IV to I). This is traditionally considered to be a progression that one might sing 'Amen' to in church, and sounds potentially more solemn than the perfect cadence. It is equally conclusive.

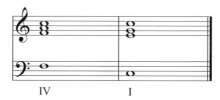

IV   I

3. Interrupted cadence

The interrupted cadence plays a trick on your sense of anticipation. It starts on chord V, and leads you to expect the finality of a perfect cadence; however, in an interrupted cadence, some other chord is used instead of chord I, often chord VI. This leads to a sense of open-endedness and the need for more music to follow. In this way it is a little like a colon in a sentence: you know there's more to come.

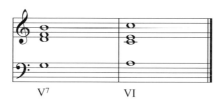

V⁷   VI

4. Imperfect cadence

Imperfect cadences are the most common kind, and their impact is the least dramatic of the four types of cadence. In these ways they are the musical equivalent of a comma. There are many different versions, but they all have in common that the second chord in the progression is chord V.

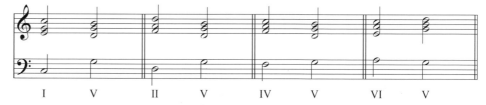

I   V   II   V   IV   V   VI   V

There is one other special feature to listen out for. Sometimes a piece in a minor key will end on the tonic chord, as you might expect, but this final chord will be the tonic major chord instead of the tonic minor chord you have heard throughout the piece.

When this occurs it is called a **Tierce de picardie**. Both perfect and plagal cadences can finish on a Tierce de picardie; the effect is very striking, and often has a dash of nobility or relief to it after a long piece in a minor key.

PEDALS AND DRONES

© www.shutterstock.com

A drone is a continuous note, usually heard in the bass. This may be familiar from hearing bagpipes playing (especially in Scotland). It is also an important feature of much music from India where several lute-like instruments contain a drone, including the tambura, the sitar, the sarangi and the sarod.

None of the standard orchestral instruments of western music has this drone feature, but this hasn't stopped composers over the ages from exploring a similar effect.

It is almost unheard of for a classical piece of music to have the same bass note all the way through, like a drone; however, it is very common for there to be passages of a few bars in which the bass note stays the same. This is called a **pedal note**.

Usually pedal notes are either the tonic or the dominant note of the home key. Early on in his *Pathétique* Sonata in C minor, Beethoven uses the tonic option to underpin his first main theme:

Allegro molto e con brio

Beethoven: Piano sonata No. 8, Op. 13 *'Pathétique'*, first movement

As a composer, one of the great benefits of using a pedal note is that at some point there will be a dramatic moment when the pedal changes note.

Exercise 14

Test yourself on harmony with these ten questions:

1. Which of these intervals is not consonant: 3rd, 5th, 6th, 7th?
2. Which note will be at the bottom of a D major chord in first inversion?
3. Which note will be at the bottom of a B minor chord in second inversion?
4. Which four notes will be in the dominant 7th chord of F major?
5. Which four notes will be in the dominant 7th chord of D minor?
6. Which two chords are required for a perfect cadence in E♭ major?
7. Which two chords are required for a plagal cadence in B♭ major?
8. If a piece in C minor ends with a tierce de picardie, on which chord will it end?
9. Which note will be in the bass if a piece in G major has a dominant pedal?
10. Which of these intervals is not dissonant: 2nd, 4th, 5th, 7th?

TEXTURE

Considering texture is a way of looking at music to see what is happening at the same time. At any one moment there might be five notes being played; just seeing those five notes in isolation may allow us to analyse what harmony is being produced, but the function of each note will not be evident.

Only by looking a little more broadly at what is going on might we realise that one note belongs to a melody high in the treble, two are part of an accompanimental figuration in the alto, another belongs to a secondary melody in the tenor, and the final one is part of a slow-moving bass line. This is texture.

Various common types of texture are described by specific terms which you should learn.

SINGLE MELODY LINE

The simplest type of texture is to have a single note at any one time. This is most likely to be part of an unaccompanied, or single melody line. Elgar uses this texture early on in his cello concerto when he first presents the main theme on the violas. Lulu's 1965 version of *Shout* opens with a single melody line.

OCTAVES

The next most straightforward of textures is to have a single line played in octaves. A famous example is the opening of Bach's Toccata in D minor where both hands play the same melody an octave apart. Try to develop your ear to hear the difference between this and just a single melody line.

MELODY WITH ACCOMPANIMENT

A lot of music presents a melody – usually at the top of the texture – with some form of accompaniment using other notes. A simple example of this is the opening to Mozart's C major piano sonata, K. 545.

Mozart: Piano sonata in C, K. 545

This is a simple example: the accompaniment (in a broken chord figuration known as Alberti bass) has only one note at a time in support of the melody. The slow movement of Beethoven's *Pathétique* sonata in C minor has a richer texture with initially two notes at a time in the accompaniment and, after eight bars, three notes at a time. In Vivaldi's 'Winter' concerto from *Le quattro stagioni* (Four Seasons), the melody in the solo violin part is supported by a texture in four parts.

HOMOPHONIC

A homophonic texture occurs when there are several parts being played or sung simultaneously and each has the same rhythm so that they change note at the same time. The most typical example of homophony is a simple hymn tune in four parts. A more elaborate example is the slow introduction to Beethoven's *Pathétique* sonata in C minor, second movement.

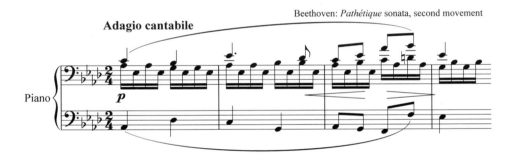

Beethoven: *Pathétique* sonata, second movement

CONTRAPUNTAL AND POLYPHONIC

Contrapuntal and polyphonic textures will have several notes occurring at the same time, but rather than one being part of an important melodic line and the others being involved in an accompanimental role, each will belong to a melodic line of more or less equal importance. A good way of looking at it is that these textures comprise several melodic strands that are woven together to make the overall musical fabric.

IMITATION AND CANON

In a contrapuntal texture, with several melodic strands being involved simultaneously, it is possible for one to copy what another has just done in some way. This is known as imitation. Usually the section imitated will be only a bar or two, but just occasionally the process becomes a structural principle for a long section of music.

In the final movement of his violin sonata, Cesar Franck (1822–1890) has the violin and piano playing the same tune, but with one instrument one bar behind the other. Initially it is the piano that leads:

This technique is known as canon: two parts play the same melodic line but starting at a different point and overlapping. Sometimes in a canon the following part plays the melody at a different pitch as well (here in the Franck example, the canon is at a higher octave in the violin).

ANTIPHONAL

An antiphonal texture requires two groups of musicians who take it in turns to play in a kind of musical conversation. Originally this was applied to sacred music in which two choirs would be involved. The term can be applied to a range of musical scenarios, however; for instance, a passage of orchestra music in which the strings section is alternating with the wind section, or a passage of rock music in which the guitars alternate with the drums.

TIMBRE

Timbre is the musician's word for describing the actual quality of sound in the way any given note is produced. Thus a 'middle C' on a violin sounds different to the same note played by an oboe.

INSTRUMENTAL CATEGORIES

The range of musical instruments throughout the world's traditions of music is good evidence both of human ingenuity and the desire to make music wherever some form of civilisation has taken root.

Try to develop the ability to identify different instruments from the sound they make. There are a limited number of technologies that can be used to produce musical sound. These sound quite clearly different, but each has been adapted into several different instruments, and hearing the difference between these can be more challenging.

As always, it is best to hear music played live rather than depending solely on recordings, so take time to listen to your friends playing whatever instruments they learn and ask them questions about how the instrument is played and what effects are possible.

The main categories of instruments are:

1. **Stringed instruments** produce sound with strings which are set to vibrate by the musician; an important aspect is the hollow box underneath the strings which allows the musical note to resonate and gain volume. There are three subcategories:

   - Bowed strings: this includes the familiar western instruments such as violin, viola, cello and double bass which are the mainstay of the symphony orchestra as well as sometimes appearing in some jazz styles and as a backing sound in pop music. There are some bowed string instruments in other music traditions in the world, such as the Chinese huqin family (including the erhu).
   - Plucked string instruments: the main western members of this instrumental category are the harp, guitar, lute and mandolin. (The bowed instruments such as the violin can, of course, be plucked too.) There are many plucked string instruments around the world including the kora from Mali (a type of harp), the various Indian lutes such as the sitar, sarangi and tambura, and the South American charango (not dissimilar from the mandolin).
   - Hammered string instruments: the least well-known of the stringed instruments are those where the strings are hit. This may be because there is little in the classical tradition for these instruments. However, in the folk music of Eastern Europe, Arabia and China, a family of instruments called dulcimers are popular. The best-known Chinese example is the yangqin.

2. **Woodwind instruments** involve a pipe which is made to resonate by blowing air down it. This stream of air needs to be focussed in some way and there are two methods of doing this:

   - Blowing across the pipe: the obvious example of this is the flute, which is held horizontally precisely so the player can blow across the instrument. The piccolo follows the same design, being a half-size flute that sounds an octave higher. Recorders achieve their sound in a similar way: although you blow down the pipe, the notch in the mouthpiece creates a similar flow of air in the main pipe.
   - Using a reed: other wind instruments require the player to make a reed vibrate. There are two versions: on a clarinet or saxophone a single reed vibrates against the mouthpiece; on oboes and bassoons, a double reed vibrates against itself.

The combination of whether the woodwind instrument uses a reed or not, and various physical properties of the pipe itself (especially whether it tapers),

© www.shutterstock.com

Mandolin

© www.shutterstock.com

Clarinet

means that each of the western wind instruments has a very distinctive timbre. Make sure you can tell them apart.

3. **Brass instruments** are not so different from woodwind instruments, in that they require wind to create sound. However, the focussing of the sound requires the player to 'buzz' their lips. Different tensions in the player's lips while doing this will change the pitch of the note being played due to some physical properties of sound which we need not go into here. Essentially, the same principle is used for all members of the brass family: cornet, trumpet, horn, trombone, tuba and others. The design of each instrument, however, means that the resulting timbres are different, from the bright trumpets to the more mellow horn. Again, you should learn to distinguish between them.

4. **Percussion instruments** are the most diverse of the instrumental categories. They have in common the method of playing: for the most part, all these instruments are hit. However, the sounds are very different, including some instruments that are tuned to play pitched notes, and many that are just a particular timbre that gives a special tone colour in a rhythmic manner. Among the main subcategories are:

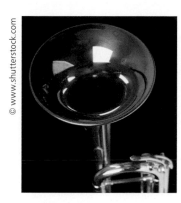
Trumpet

Glockenspiel

Balafon

The technical name for drums is 'membranophones'.

- **Drums**: These come in a bewildering array of shapes and sizes, and fulfil a wide range of roles from a military marching band to a jazz combo. They share the properties of a tightened skin over a confined space that makes the sound resonate. Among the drums in world music traditions you will meet are the African djembe and the Indian tabla. The orchestral timpani of western classical music are notable in that they are tuned to play specific pitches: often the tonic and dominant of the music.
- **Tuned mallet percussion**: there are a range of percussion instruments which have a series of bars, each tuned to a different note, which are struck by sticks or mallets. In the orchestra the most common are the xylophone (wooden bars that sound very dry and brittle) and the glockenspiel (metal bars with a very pure ringing tone). In jazz one sometimes hears the shimmering tone of the vibraphone, and from the Latin American tradition there is the marimba which is now a specialist solo percussion instrument in the western tradition. A similar instrument from Mali is the balafon which is made with empty gourds under the bars to give an attractive hollow timbre. Somewhat different are the Caribbean steel pans, where oil drums are fashioned so that different dimples in the surface of the drums play different pitched notes.
- **Shakers and scrapers**: These instruments make a distinctive rasp or rattle and include maracas, which are shaken, and the guiro, which is scraped.
- **Other untuned percussion**: most of the other percussion instruments sometimes found in an orchestra do not have specific pitch but are used for the distinctive timbre they bring when struck. Listen out for the difference between the resonant, long-lasting sounds from metal

Organ

Electric guitar

instruments such as the cymbals, tam-tam (or gong) and triangle, and compare this to the dry, short sound of wooden instruments such as the wood block, claves and castanets.

5. **Keyboard instruments:** this final category of acoustic instruments, though it has few really well-known members, is perhaps the most diverse. Although the method of playing the instruments (via a keyboard with your fingers) is similar, the way the sound is produced differs greatly, and so does the timbre. With the piano, strings are hit by hammers; on the harpsichord strings are plucked by quills; meanwhile the organ produces its timbres by pressurized air by released up through pipes.

6. **Electronic instruments**: advances in technology over the past half-century or so have brought about a revolution in the instrumental options available to musicians. At first, the main widely adopted advance was in the possibility that a 'pick-up' could be attached to a string instrument. This has included using such a device on a string bass in jazz combos, and to the electric violin used in some modern pop styles. The main innovation, though, has been the electric guitar, the mainstay of rock music. More recently, developments in digital technology have led to remarkable new potential for sampled sounds that can be manipulated using computers. Much of the modern music industry, including film music, makes wide use of this area.

SPECIAL INSTRUMENTAL TECHNIQUES

Most instruments have some special playing techniques that vary their timbre. An exhaustive list would take considerable space, and composers are imaginative people who are always on the lookout for new innovative sounds. The following selective list has common instrumental techniques, which you should be able to identify from the relevant sound:

- **Con sordini** (bowed strings): A device called a mute is clipped onto the bridge, limiting the available vibration of the instrument and therefore dulling the tone, creating a more distant and doleful sound.
- **Pizzicato** (bowed strings): This instruction tells the players to pluck the strings rather than bowing them, changing the timbre completely from a sustained, lyrical tone to a short, incisive sound with only brief resonance.
- **Arco** (bowed strings): An instruction to resume playing with bows after a passage of pizzicato.
- **Tremolo/Tremolando** (bowed strings): Requires players to rapidly move the bow back and forth on the string instead of a single bowstroke for the duration of a note; the result is a shimmering sound.

- **Con sordini** (brass): The brass version of a mute is inserted into the bell of the instrument, to produce a more muffled tone that can sound very nasal and pinched when played loudly.

VOICES AND VOCAL TECHNIQUES

One of the joys of singing is that every voice is unique and can only be used by one human being. Nevertheless, various categories of voice are common:

- **Soprano**: the highest female voice
- **Treble**: a boy's voice before 'breaking'; the equivalent range to a soprano
- **Alto**: a lower female voice
- **Countertenor**: a male voice of alto range, achieved by a man singing falsetto (see below)
- **Tenor**: a high male voice (without singing falsetto)
- **Bass**: the lowest male voice.

There are some special vocal techniques to listen out for:

- **Falsetto**: this is an unusual way for the adult male to sing, that concentrates the resonance in the head (as opposed to the chest) and creates a very pure timbre. It is most commonly found in performances of Baroque choral music and cathedral choirs.
- **Portamento**: this is a technique that involves sliding between two notes rather than an instant change of pitch. Listen out for it especially in operatic singing.
- **Vibrato**: this is the use of some slight variation of pitch such that the note pulsates a little, intensifying the sound. Many instruments, especially bowed stringed instruments, use vibrato, but it is particularly effective in operatic singing.

TECHNOLOGY AND TIMBRE

One of the advantages of the new electronic timbres is that the sound can be instantaneously passed through various units to manipulate the timbre further. This is a very technical area of music, but a few particular techniques that you need to be able to recognise are:

- **Reverb**: this is, effectively, a way of electronically adding an echo effect to the sound, so that it sounds as though it is being played in a large, resonant room.
- **Distortion**: this can just mean the alteration of the original timbre electronically, but it is particularly associated with the aggressive timbre available on the electric guitar and used in heavy rock music.
- **Chorus**: this manipulates the sound to give the impression that it is being produced by multiple sources, thereby imitating a string ensemble or choir, for example.

DYNAMICS AND TIMBRE

Dynamic is the musician's word for volume. However, this has more influence than just turning up the volume on your stereo, it also changes the intensity of the sound and so changing dynamics can affect the timbre of many instruments. For example, the flute can sound quite shrill and piercing at its loudest volume, but sweet and mellifluous when played softly.

It is important that you know the various symbols for dynamics:

- *pp* means pianissimo, or very soft
- *p* means piano, or soft
- *mp* means mezzo-piano, or moderately soft
- *mf* means mezzo-forte, or moderately loud
- *f* means forte, or loud
- *ff* means fortissimo, or very loud
- crescendo (or *cresc.*) means get louder; an alternative sign is ⏜
- diminuendo (or *dim.*) means get softer; an alternative sign is ⏝

STRUCTURE AND FORM

The final area of study requires you to think about the overall shape of a piece of music. Without consideration being given to this aspect of a piece, it is hard for a listener to follow where the music is leading.

There are various factors that play an important role in the structure of most pieces:

- What melodic ideas are played
- What keys are used
- When contrast is made, perhaps through texture, instrumentation, rhythmic character or dynamic
- When an earlier idea returns
- What unifying factors may be used through the piece.

BINARY FORM

Binary form is usually used for a short movement, and was popular in the 18th century for pieces based on old dances, such as **Allemandes**, **Gigues** and **Menuets**.

As the name implies, there are two sections. These are of approximately equal length and often have matching (or 'rhyming') final cadences. The opening to each half may also show some similarities. Each half usually repeats and is played twice.

An important factor is that the first section usually modulates to the dominant; the second half then returns the music to the tonic.

The form can be represented as follows:

A (x2)	B (x2)
Tonic modulating to dominant	Dominant modulating back to tonic

The Haydn Menuet on page 44 above shows all these common factors of binary form.

TERNARY FORM

Ternary form is one of the most versatile of musical forms. It comprises three sections. The first is a self-contained paragraph of music which begins and ends in the same key. The second section is contrasting, especially through being in a different key. The final section is usually the same as the first (though may have some changes). This may be represented as follows:

A	B	A
Tonic	Contrasting key	Tonic

A very wide range of pieces have used ternary form, including arias from Baroque operas, Menuet and Trios in Classical symphonies, and 19th-century characteristic pieces for piano.

RONDO

Rondo was a popular form of Classical period composers, who sometimes used the structure for the final movement of a sonata. There is a self-contained main theme (the Rondo theme) which begins and ends in the same key (the tonic). This appears several times, and always in the tonic. In between come contrasting sections (episodes) which use other, related keys. The form may be represented as follows:

A	B	A	C	A	D	A
Tonic	Related key	Tonic	Related key	Tonic	Related key	Tonic

The final movement of Beethoven's *Pathétique* sonata in C minor is a rondo.

THEME AND VARIATIONS

Theme and variations was another form enjoyed especially by Classical period composers, often as the second movement in a sonata or string quartet. A short, self-contained passage of music presents the main theme for the movement. There then follow several further sections, where the music of the theme is treated to a series of variations in which the theme is changed in some way. Aspects of the theme that could be changed in variations include:

- The melodic line, often through ornamentation and decoration
- The texture
- The metre
- The tempo
- The key, often including the tonic minor for a theme in a major key.

 Listening ideas

Two fine sets of variations are:

- Haydn: String quartet in C major, Op. 76 No. 3, 'Emperor', second movement
- Schubert: Piano quintet in A major, D. 667, 'Trout', fourth movement.

SONATA

Sonatas for instruments such as the violin usually include a piano accompaniment.

The word 'sonata' is applied both to a type of piece and a specific form. The sonata as a piece really came of age in the Classical period, when it became established as the premier large-scale piece for a solo instrument, especially the piano.

The plan for a sonata was, traditionally, to have three separate pieces, called 'movements'. The first movement would be the most substantial and usually quite quick (although there might be a slow introduction). The second movement, probably in a different, but related, key, would be a slow movement. The last movement, or 'finale', would be in the same key as the first movement and very quick.

Of these three movements, the first movement was usually structured in what is now known as 'sonata form'. Whole books have been written on this form: it is one of the most important in music. Suffice for now to say that this long movement would be in three sections:

- Section 1, called the **exposition**, has two main themes and ends in the dominant
- Section 2, called the **development**, explores the potential of these themes in a variety of keys and sounds very much like the middle of the piece
- Section 3, called the **recapitulation**, is very similar to the exposition, but stays in the tonic.

Not only sonatas are based on sonata form: many symphonies, concertos, overtures and even Mass settings use it too.

MINUET AND TRIO

The instruction for the Minuet to be played again after the Trio is the Italian 'da capo' at the end of the Trio, meaning 'from the head'.

Minuet and Trio (sometimes spelled 'Menuet') is the traditional third movement of a Classical period symphony. Minuets were elegant dances of the 18th century that were in triple time and played at a moderate tempo. They tended to be quite short movements in binary form. The trio is, effectively, another Minuet that will contrast in some way with the first: it is usually somewhat slighter with a less full texture. After the Trio, the original Minuet is played again; convention is that the repeats are not played this time.

Virtually all of Haydn's 104 symphonies have a Minuet and Trio. In the 19th century the Minuet was replaced by a Scherzo and Trio: a rather more substantial piece.

GROUND BASS

Ground bass was a form popular in the mid-Baroque era (the second half of the 17th century). A bass line of up to around eight bars is repeated many times over while the upper parts of the texture play more varied lines.

Master of the ground bass was the English composer Henry Purcell. Perhaps his most famous example is the aria 'When I am laid in Earth' from his opera *Dido and Aeneas*, with its mournful chromatically-descending bass line for the ground tune.

CONCERTO

Wolfgang Amadeus Mozart

A concerto is a substantial piece for a solo instrument accompanied by orchestra. Vivaldi was one of the earliest great composers of concertos, and in writing over 200 of them he did much to establish the form. Usually there are three movements: fast – slow – fast.

The concerto was a favourite of Mozart who wrote many fine examples especially with piano as the solo instrument. An important feature from this point on was the **cadenza**. This was a long and virtuosic passage for the soloist alone, while the orchestra rested. Usually this comes on the final cadence before the orchestral coda to the first movement (cadence and cadenza are obviously similar words).

POPULAR SONG FORMS

No genre of music is more diverse than songs. Space here allows only a brief mention of three particular structural plans:

1. **Call and response**: This is a common device in many traditions of world music, but especially in African music. Typically there is a leader who sings each phrase first (the 'call'); the chorus then repeat each phrase directly afterwards (the 'response'). The beauty of this system is that no one needs copies of the music: so long as the leader knows the song, everyone else only has to listen and copy in order to be able to join in.

> A simple definition of 32-bar song form is AABA'.

2. **32-bar song form**: This is the form most common in music theatre. A melody is constructed in four long phrases (traditionally eight bars each, though this can vary). The second phrase is almost the same as the first, though the cadences are likely to differ; the third phrase offers some contrast, a new idea; the final phrase reverts to the opening tune, but probably changes the ending somehow. 'On the street where you live' from *My Fair Lady* is one fine example of thousands of this form.

3. **Pop ballad**: There are many variants of how to write a rock or pop song, but a common general model is as follows: intro, verse, chorus, verse, chorus, instrumental, chorus, outro. Elton John's song 'Sacrifice' follows this plan. Listen to some of your favourite songs and see whether or not they are structured this way.

THE WESTERN CLASSICAL TRADITION

The Western Classical Tradition is an immense range of music with many diverse styles and spanning over 1,000 years of human musical activity. From all this, AQA have selected five particular areas for you to explore:

- Baroque orchestral music
- The concerto
- Music for voices
- Chamber music
- The sonata.

There are no compulsory works to study. Rather, you should look at enough examples from each category (and there is no shortage of wonderful music from which to choose) to understand how composers used all the elements of music (as outlined in the Areas of Study) to create each distinctive genre and style of music.

You will be expected to use the understanding you build up from this exploration of these repertoires to respond critically to the music you will be played in the Unit 1 exam. The chances are that you will not have heard this music before, but if you have studied a representative sample from each area, you should be fine.

In this book, we look at a representative sample of music for each 'Strand'. This may include pieces you listen to in class, in which case this book can serve as a reminder of what you have learned, or may be additional to the music your teacher uses, in which case this book will help to broaden your musical experience and understanding.

Keywords:

Genre: literally means category, used to describe types of piece such as concerto, sonata, symphony, suite, mass, opera, musical, soundtrack and so on.

Style: used to describe the way the elements of music are used together to form a distinctive flavour of musical language, such as Baroque, Classical, Romantic, jazz, blues, R'n'B, hip hop and so on.

 ## Resources

Of course, the most important thing is how the music actually sounds. Various specific recordings will be mentioned, but much is available online. Among the sites you might check out are:

- The Naxos Music Library at www.naxosmusiclibrary.com: superb for many styles of music, above all the western classical tradition. See if your school or college subscribes, and, if not, suggest that they do so.
- www.youtube.com: a good resource for contemporary music videos and an eclectic mix of other musical recordings.
- www.spotify.com: for streaming music through the internet
- www.itunes.com: for downloading music from the iTunes store.

Introduction

The Baroque period covers the period from around 1600 to 1750. In many ways it is a watershed age in the history of music. Among other notable factors:

- It was an age in which secular music flourished to a point of near-equality with the sacred music that had dominated earlier centuries. This was, perhaps, due in part to the continuing effects of the Reformation in Europe.
- It saw the rise of opera in Italy, notably with works by Monteverdi based on classical mythology, such as *Orfeo*.
- It was the first period in which instrumental music really blossomed, in conjunction with developments in instrument-making, including the fine organs that J. S. Bach played, and the violins of the superb Antonio Stradivari, whose violins to this day are widely considered the greatest ever made.
- It was the period in which **tonality** became established as the accepted system for organising pitch, taking over from the **modality** of the previous Renaissance style.

The word 'baroque' is thought to derive from the Portuguese word *barroco*, meaning a pearl of irregular shape, and is often associated with the manufacture of jewellery. Certainly, in music, the Baroque style is usually ornate, often involving sophisticated compositional techniques such as:

- Complex contrapuntal textures that often involve several layers and much imitation
- An interest in rich instrumental colours, especially a high-pitched trumpet
- Intricate melodic lines that are propelled forwards with immense rhythmic vigour
- Expressive use of suspensions and chromatic inflections in the harmony.

These factors can combine to create spectacular and glittering effects.

The Baroque orchestra

The orchestra essentially came into existence in the 17th century. Before this period instrumentalists would play together, but usually in small groups. In the earlier part of the Baroque period there were a growing number of occasions on which such groups would play. These included:

- Playing for operas in Italy, e.g. Monteverdi's *Orfeo* in 1607
- Playing at court, e.g. the '24 violons du Roi' employed at the court of Louis XIII in France by 1618
- Accompanying music in church, e.g. Biber's *Missa salisburgensis* written for Salzburg Cathedral in 1682.

In the final two decades of the 17th century these various bands evolved into something much more recognisable as an orchestra: strings, and especially violins, were increasingly seen to be the backbone of the orchestra, and the old-fashioned renaissance wind instruments (like shawms and cornets) disappeared and were replaced by recorders, flutes, oboes and bassoons.

The term 'orchestra' comes from the word for the area in front of the stage in ancient Greece: the place where the musicians sat.

Antonio Vivaldi

The music you are likely to study for this topic, therefore, comes from the final part of the Baroque period in the first half of the 18th century. There are, perhaps, three main composers to look out for:

- Antonio Vivaldi: writing in Italy, notably Venice
- Johann Sebastian Bach: writing in northern Germany
- George Frideric Handel: German composer, who visited Italy and then settled in England.

Vivaldi: 'Winter' from *Le quattro stagioni (The Four Seasons)*

Vivaldi's set of four violin concertos called *The Four Seasons* are among the most popular and most recorded of all classical works. They were first published among a set of 12 concertos entitled 'Il cimento dell'armonia e dell'inventione' ('The contest between harmony and invention').

Like its companion concertos, 'Winter' comprises three movements in a kind of sandwich: a slow movement in the middle with two fast movements on the outside. Each of the concertos is intended to capture the scenes painted by a sonnet (or poem) about the season. Here is the sonnet for 'Winter', with an English translation, showing which lines go with each of the three movements:

Italian	English
First movement: *Aggiacciato tremar trà nevi algenti* *Al Severo Spirar d'orrido Vento,* *Correr battendo i piedi ogni momento;* *E pel Soverchio gel batter i denti.*	To tremble from cold in the icy snow, In the harsh breath of a horrid wind; To run, stamping one's feet every moment, Our teeth chattering in the extreme cold.
Second movement: *Passar al foco i di quieti e contenti* *Mentre la pioggia fuor bagna ben cento.*	Before the fire to pass peaceful, Contented days while the rain outside pours down.
Third movement: *Caminar Sopra il giaccio, e à passo lento* *Per timor di cader gersene intenti;* *Gir forte Sdruzziolar, cader à terra* *Di nuove ir Sopra 'l giaccio e correr forte* *Sin ch' il giaccio si rompe, e si disserra;* *Sentir uscir dalle ferrate porte* *Sirocco Borea, e tutti i Venti in guerra* *Quest' é 'l verno, mà tal, che gioia apporte.*	We tread the icy path slowly and cautiously, for fear of tripping and falling. Then turn abruptly, slip, crash on the ground and, rising, hasten on across the ice lest it cracks up. We feel the chill north winds course through the home despite the locked and bolted doors... this is winter, which nonetheless brings its own delights.

The concerto is written for a solo violinist accompanied by a small orchestra of string players in four teams: first violins, second violins, violas and cellos.

If you have chance to follow a score, you will see each part on its own stave; you may also notice two unusual details regarding the cellos' stave: it is also labelled as being for organ as well as cellos, and there is a series of numbers under the stave.

All this is actually quite usual for Baroque orchestral music. In this style, the strings are supported by some kind of harmonic instrument, normally a keyboard instrument such as a harpsichord or organ. The player follows the cello part, playing these notes in the left hand, and converts the numbers into chords: each number informs the player of notes that are in the chord at that point.

The numbers are called **figured bass.**

The combination of cello and keyboard instrument in this way is known as **basso continuo**.

The piece is in the suitably dark and wintry key of F minor, with four flats in the key signature.

Let's look at some of the details of the music:

First movement

The opening 11 bars paint a vivid picture of an icy scene. There is no real melody; instead the texture builds from a single bass note in bar 1, to a four-note chord in bar 4.

The frozen character is present from the start with the detached repeating quavers (bowed in pairs). The entry of the violas on a dissonant G in bar 2 (while the cellos stay on the keynote of F) adds to the tension, and the D♭ in bar 3 and B♭ in bar 4 reinforce this. The trills in the solo violin part seem like a wintry shiver.

The chord progression moves to the dominant of C minor by bar 12. Here the orchestra breaks off, and the solo violin plays a dazzling line of demi-semiquavers representing the winter wind. Note how this melodic line comprises…

■ Arpeggios
■ Scales
■ Triadic writing
■ A final long trill.

… all features typical of Baroque melodic writing.

Vivaldi: *Winter*, first movement

The music maintains the same mood until bar 22 when there is a sudden eruption that portrays the stamping of feet in the sonnet:

Vivaldi: *Winter*, first movement

This is a thrilling passage, and one of great harmonic significance. Follow the bass line: the C falls to F which is a 5th lower; now take the higher F and see that this falls another 5th to Bb; this falls to Eb which is a 5th lower, and the higher Eb falls to Ab, which is another 5th lower. In fact, every move in the bass is a fall of a 5th. This results in a special, very effective, chord sequence known as a circle of 5ths: see how closely it follows the diagram of keys on page 41.

The impact of this special chord sequence is reinforced by the energy in the rhythm and the conformity of the texture: with every instrument doing something similar, the texture here can be described as homophonic.

The remainder of this first movement is constructed from similar material to the passages we have already discussed.

Second movement

It is not only the change of tempo that allows this second movement to provide contrast. It is in a different key, and a major one at that: Eb major.

The movement is only 18 bars long, but there is an exquisite sense of design here: the music is in two halves, with a perfect cadence in the dominant key of Bb at bar 8 matched by a perfect cadence back in the tonic key of Eb major in bar 16 (followed by two bars that are almost a forerunner of modern 'fade-out' endings).

The texture is fascinating – every instrument has a specific role:

- Solo violin: plays a lyrical and expressive melody
- First and second violins: play pizzicato broken chord patterns
- Violas: play long, sustained harmony notes
- Cellos: play repeated quavers on the bass line.

The resulting music captures perfectly the fireside contentment of the sonnet's lines for this section of the concerto.

The melody is largely conjunct, but has some all-important leaps that bring definition to the contour. The most memorable line in the first half of the movement has a rising scale that is treated to a falling sequence, each new scale starting a 7th lower than the end of the previous one:

To give further balance to the movement, in the second half the same rising melodic shape is treated to a rising sequence:

Third movement

There are some interesting features in this final movement of 'Winter'. The texture for the first 20 bars is very sparse: just the solo violin melody and a single sustained note in the cello.

The violin melody is a long line of constant semiquavers, using a repetition technique of several bars. The sustained cello note, on the tonic F, is a pedal note. When the cello does change note, at bar 21, it is to the dominant (C) for another long pedal note.

Much of the melodic material is scalic, until, at bar 73, there is some flamboyant string-crossing figuration for the soloist.

Handel: Concerto grosso in D minor, Op. 3 No. 5

Vivaldi's *Four Seasons* are concertos for solo violin, accompanied by a small orchestra. The concerto grosso was an alternative kind of concerto, which disappeared after the Baroque period. Here there is no one musician who is the soloist: the ensemble as a whole is important, although several players may continue to play at times when the remainder of the orchestra take a rest.

Handel published his set of six opus 3 concerti grossi in London in 1734. This fifth one of the set is in D minor, and is in five sections or movements. It is scored for oboes and strings, a standard small-scale Baroque orchestra. Notice that the bass line in the score is again intended for continuo: it is probable that cellos, a double bass and the harpsichordist (or organist) would be following this line; there are once again figures on this bass line to help the keyboard player.

First movement

There is no tempo marking in the score here, but a steady speed suits this rather solemn music with its mostly sinking chord progression – follow the cello part as it descends through an octave scale from bar 2.

An attractive feature of this opening movement is the way rhythm, texture and register are used in an alternating pattern. On the first downbeat there is a full chord of the tonic D minor. Then the two violin parts in unison play a rising scale in triplet quavers that has the 'kick' start of a quaver rest. This violin line is unaccompanied, i.e. it is just a single melody line. Though this is a rising scale pattern, the final note on the downbeat of the next bar is a leap downwards. Then on the second beat of the second bar the chords return with a dotted pattern in duple rhythm to contrast with the melodic triplets.

Single melodic line in low register with triplet rhythms　Homophonic chords in high register, duplet rhythm

Handel: Concerto grosso in D minor, Op. 3 No. 5

There is a very clear example of a hemiola rhythm at bars 23–24 as the music cadences into C major (note the B♮s):

The movement ends with an imperfect cadence onto the dominant chord of A major ready for the next movement.

Second movement: Allegro

Compared to the first movement, this is a more contrapuntal movement: there are often three independent melodic parts playing at the same time, although the violas double the cellos throughout at an octave above.

All the important material for the movement is presented in the first four bars. There are three elements to track through the movement:

- ■ The bold two-bar phrase heard unaccompanied in the first violin comprising a falling scale and a rising 6th
- ■ The disjunct pattern of seven quavers in bar 3
- ■ The falling conjunct pattern in tied crotchets in the oboes and second violins.

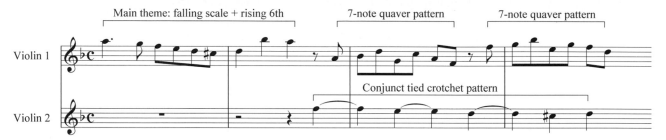

Follow through the movement and see how Handel maintains the momentum with the quaver pattern and builds the whole movement from these three elements. Occasionally the texture reduces to just two parts, but this allows for a significant entry of the main theme when the third part re-enters, such as the cellos in bar 54.

Three bars before the end there is an interrupted cadence followed by a short gap, before a final Adagio cadence to end the movement.

Third movement: Adagio

This is a short and expressive slow movement with some expressive melodic writing. Listen out for how the two top lines are so close together that they often leap-frog each other (e.g. bar 3). The bass line (doubled by the violas at a higher octave) is some way away in the texture; it is the job of the keyboard continuo player to fill this gap in the texture with their 'realisation' of the figured bass.

Fourth movement: Allegro, ma non troppo

This is another contrapuntal movement in three parts with the violas doubling the cellos. The main melodic idea is an energetic one, its momentum coming from the initial octave leap and the tie halfway through that gives a kick to the rhythm:

Like the previous Allegro movement the music breaks off just before the end, this time with an imperfect cadence, and, after the short gap, there is a brief Adagio for the closing perfect cadence to the movement.

Fifth movement: Allegro

This unusual final movement is in $\frac{2}{2}$ time, and starts halfway through a bar, rather like a Gavotte does (see page 74). There is a huge sense of propulsion here as all instruments charge forwards together from the start, playing essentially in octaves for the first 12 bars. When the music then first breaks into a three-part texture, there is imitation between the violins and the cellos, who are a beat behind.

There seems to be little respite from the forward thrust of the music, with the reliance on conjunct crotchets creating a double quick march feel, energised by the groups of four quavers every so often. However, the music does modulate and cadence in some related keys: the relative major or F major at bars 29–30, and the dominant of A minor at bars 43–44.

Listen out for the change of texture from bar 56 where the second violins are separated from the rest of the orchestra in an antiphonal passage.

There is a perfect cadence in the tonic (D minor) at bars 73–74. This, however, is only the end of the first section: a middle section of 24 bars follows which starts in F major, passes through C major, and ends in A minor. There is then the instruction *da capo* and the whole of the first section (74 bars) is played again. This creates a ternary form movement: ABA, where the A section is self-contained starting and finishing in the tonic key, and the B section is in a contrasting key (or, in this case, keys).

Bach: Orchestral Suite No. 3 in D major

Johann Sebastian Bach

A suite is a collection of short pieces, which are mostly types of dance. Sometimes there is a more extended movement at the start. Bach wrote many different suites, some for harpsichord, and other for various string instruments including violin, cello and lute. In addition, Bach wrote four suites for orchestra; this third suite was probably written between 1729 and 1731.

All the movements of the suite are in D major. This is significant because in the Baroque era it was one of the few keys in which trumpets could play. It was still nearly 100 years before instrument makers invented valves for brass instruments; without valves the trumpet only had a restricted number of notes available. This had two important implications:

■ The music needed to be in a key that made this limited range of notes useful; therefore composers usually wrote in D major when they wanted to use trumpets.
■ More notes were available in the trumpet's top register, so trumpet parts tend to be high in Baroque music; in mid register only the notes of the tonic arpeggio are available.

Notes available for a Baroque trumpet in C:

In Baroque orchestral music, wherever there are trumpets in use, there are usually timpani too, playing the tonic and dominant notes of the key. In addition Bach writes for two oboes as well as the usual strings and continuo.

In total there are six movements:

- Overture
- Air
- Gavotte I
- Gavotte II
- Bourrée
- Gigue.

First movement: Overture

This majestic opening movement is of a particular type found only in Baroque music and called a French overture. Usually there are two sections:

First section	Second section
Slow – often Grave	Fast – probably Allegro
Prominent dotted rhythm patterns	Contrapuntal – probably fugal
Ends on chord V	Ends on the tonic
Is repeated	

Listen through this movement and you will soon find plenty of evidence for saying this is a French overture: the opening section is 24 bars long and grandiose with plenty of dotted rhythms that, at a slow tempo, create a sense of formality. The opening is spectacular with its long timpani roll and the three trumpet parts.

Keep an ear open for what happens in the bass line: it may be static for two long, slow bars (in fact there is a tonic pedal here) but thereafter the bass line is very active – a common feature in music by Bach. The bass is particularly busy at the end of the opening section as it approaches the imperfect cadence that is typical at this point of a French overture.

After the repeat the music doubles the tempo for the second section, and a new tune with a driving rhythm of a repeating pattern comprising two semiquavers and a quaver is heard. This is played by first violins and first oboe, in unison, as a single melody line. When the second violins and second oboe join in it is with the same tune though from a different pitch; meanwhile the first violins and first oboe move to a secondary tune in quavers and involving ties:

Main theme, called the fugue subject, starting on A (first violin / first oboe)

Secondary idea, called the countersubject

Main theme, now starting on D (second violin / second oboe)

One-bar extension

Violas about to enter, with subject starting on A

Soon the music is busy with these two different melodic ideas in a busy texture that is very contrapuntal. Indeed, this section can be described as being a **fugue**, a particular kind of contrapuntal composition of which Bach was the supreme master. Listen out especially for when the main fugue subject is high up in the trumpet: challenging writing for the trumpeter to play, but a scintillating effect.

Finally as the fugue comes to its final perfect cadence, Bach has a surprise in store with a return to the slow music of the opening section with its dotted rhythms. This ensures a spectacular ending to the movement.

Second movement: Air

After the grandeur of the overture, this Air provides maximum contrast. It only uses the strings and has an intimate feel to it. The movement is in binary form:

■ 'A' section: bars 1–6, starting in D major, modulating to the dominant (A major); repeated
■ 'B' section: bars 7–18, starting in A major, returning to the tonic via B minor at bar 10; also repeated.

The most obvious element of the texture is the exquisitely beautiful melody, which is quite intricate with its use of demisemiquavers at times and mix of conjunct motion with wide leaps. Next listen out for the steady quavers in the bass line which give the movement its regular tread. Finally try to catch the detail in the inner parts, the second violins and violas, which often have interesting moments when the melodic line is more static. At the start the texture could be described simply as melody line with accompaniment, but Bach's delight in contrapuntal textures means that these inner parts become increasingly significant, especially in the second half.

Third movement: Gavotte I

A Gavotte was one of numerous style of dance that were sometimes included in suites. The main features of the Gavotte are that it is quite lively and in $\frac{2}{2}$ time. Also, each phrase usually starts halfway through the bar, anticipating the stress of the next downbeat.

Like the previous Air, this Gavotte is in binary form, and it follows a similar pattern:

- ■ 'A' section: bars 1–10, staring in D major, modulating to the dominant (A major); repeated
- ■ 'B' section: bars 11–26, staring in A major, returning to the tonic via B minor at bar 18; repeated.

The movement has a very uplifting and positive mood, generated by the opening melodic shape that begins with a rising octave leap. This shape returns several times, but notice how Bach turns the shape upside down to start the 'B' section:

Start of 'A' section:

Rising octave – falling 3rd – rising step

Start of 'B' section:

Rising octave – falling 3rd – rising step

Fourth movement: Gavotte II

It is not unusual in a suite for there to be a pair of Gavottes. Here the second one has many of the same characteristics, including the binary form with a visit to B minor in the second half (at bar 24). The mood is a little more subdued, with the opening melodic idea being a falling shape that is, essentially, played in octaves by the orchestra.

At the end of this second Gavotte is the instruction 'Gavotte I da capo' which requires a reprise of the first Gavotte.

Fifth movement: Bourrée

The Bourrée has much in common with the Gavotte, using the same metre ($\frac{2}{2}$) and being played at a similar tempo. However, where the Gavotte has a minim upbeat to start each phrase, the Bourrée only has a crotchet upbeat which lends a slightly more flowing and less formal character to this dance.

This is another binary form movement, and once again there is a brief visit to the relative minor (B minor) in the second half (bar 20).

Sixth movement: Gigue

The Gigue was the normal way to complete a Baroque suite, being a high-spirited, fast dance in compound time (usually $\frac{6}{8}$). The typical quaver upbeat gives energy to the music, reinforced by the opening phrase which takes the first trumpet up to its highest note in a thrilling start:

This is a somewhat more substantial movement than the previous four in the suite, and this allows Bach to make a feature of having passages when the trumpets do not play, so that their re-entry (together with the timpani) can make an impact.

Once again there is a visit to B minor in the second half (bar 32), but also a cadence into F♯ minor at bar 48, before the music works its way home to D major.

Listening ideas

If you want to explore this topic further there is no shortage of music to hear. The following is recommended:

- Concertos: Bach – violin concertos in A minor and E major; Albinoni – oboe concertos
- Concerti grossi: Bach – 6 *Brandenburg* concertos; Corelli – 'Christmas' concerto
- Suites: Handel – *Water Music*; Roman – *Drottningholm Music*.

Introduction

The **concerto** is a substantial piece for a solo instrument accompanied by orchestra that is usually in three movements.

We have already looked at one concerto: Vivaldi's 'Winter' from *The Four Seasons*, a series of violin concertos. The concerto really came of age, however, in the classical period, especially in the hands of Mozart who wrote many examples including 27 piano concertos, and many others for solo instruments ranging from the violin to the clarinet.

The Concerto was particularly popular during the 19th century with the rise of the virtuoso performer. Some of these, especially the phenomenal violinist Paganini, and pianist Franz Liszt, used the concerto as a vehicle for demonstrating the wizardry of their playing. Developments in instrumental design also facilitated the concerto, especially where the piano was concerned, and by the later Romantic era the concerto provided a virtual battlefield for the concert grand piano to take on the full symphony orchestra, often with thrilling results.

In the 20th century the concerto has remained popular with composers and a wide range of works have appeared, including Poulenc's organ concerto, Rodrigo's guitar concerto, Vaughan Williams's tuba concerto and James MacMillan's concerto for percussion called *Veni, veni Emmanuel*.

Franz Liszt

Mozart: Horn Concerto in E♭ K. 447

Many concertos have been inspired by leading players. This was the case with the horn concertos written by Mozart in the 1780s which were written for a virtuoso horn player from Salzburg (Mozart's home town), one Joseph Leutgeb.

In Mozart's day the horn, like Bach's trumpet, was still without valves and limited in the notes that it could play. However, Leutgeb had mastered various techniques of playing this so-called 'natural horn' that made more chromatic notes available, this included pushing the hand up the bell of the instrument to alter the pitch, and being able to play a trill through highly difficult variation of pressure with the lips.

Such advances in playing technique inspired Mozart to write at least four concertos for the horn which revel in the rich timbre of the instrument. This particular concerto was written around 1787.

In addition to the solo horn, Mozart writes for an orchestra of two clarinets, two bassoons and strings.

First movement: Allegro

The design of this movement is wonderfully clever and fully of subtlety and resourcefulness. A full analysis is not necessary at GCSE, but the broad outline is a blend of old-fashioned concerto ritornello form from the Baroque days and the new sonata form of the Classical era, as follows:

1–28	29–79	80–111	112–159	160–183
Orchestral introduction	Exposition	Development	Recapitulation	Coda and cadenza

Most of the main thematic ideas for the movement are presented in the introduction. The opening four bars are typical of the Classical style:

Mozart: Horn concerto K. 447, opening, skeleton score

Note the following details:

- The first three notes of the tune outline the tonic triad
- The opening harmonic progression is I–V–I: the standard way for a Classical era piece to establish the key
- The simplicity of the accompaniment with little of interest in the inner parts
- The sense of two two-bar phrases that balance each other
- The elegance of the chromatic appoggiatura on the downbeat of bar 4
- The repeating E♭s in the bassoons in bar 4.

From these four bars alone one should be able to tell that this is a Classical period work.

The exposition follows the normal characteristics of sonata form with the second theme appearing in the dominant key (B♭ major) at bar 52, firstly in the violins and then answered by the solo horn. After this comes a phrase for the horn which captures several features of the classical style:

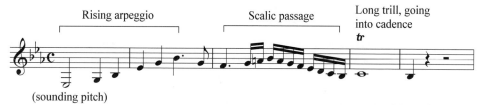

(sounding pitch)

The development section soon sounds like a middle section due to the swift departure for a remote key: D♭ major. This is done through a very simple twist from B♭ major (at the end of the development) to B♭ minor. The route back is equally cunning: see if you can hear where the change happens.

The recapitulation returns the music to E♭ major, and this time the second theme stays in this home key (bar 140).

The coda is quite substantial, breaking off at what promises to be a weighty cadence for a cadenza: a chance for the soloist to improvise an unaccompanied passage on the themes of the movement. As the soloists finishes with a trademark trill, the orchestra resume and finish the movement with a confident passage of wholly diatonic music.

Second movement: Larghetto

The slow movement of the concerto is in the subdominant key of A♭ major which has a warm glow to it. Unlike the start of the first movement, the horn has the melody from the outset. It is a beautiful, lyrical theme of eight bars that falls into the hallmark phrasing of the Classical period: four two-bar phrases of which the first and third are the same; the second phrase finishes with an imperfect cadence and the fourth with a perfect cadence:

This theme comes several times during the movement with contrasting episodes in between. Listen out especially for Mozart's uses of the clarinets and bassoons to make sustained four-note chords, in particular when they are marked with sforzandos.

Third movement: Allegro

The final movement of the concerto is a rondo structure. The main rondo theme in compound time (§) is full of good humour with its repeated quavers and chromatic passing notes:

Typically this eight-bar phrase that finished on an imperfect cadence would be followed by another matching eight-bar phrase that finishes on a perfect cadence, but Mozart's sense of fun extends this until it comes to rest on a dominant 7th chord with pause which requires a further four bars to take the music to the long-expected perfect cadence. Then Mozart gives us eight bars of just the tonic chord with an arpeggio-based melody.

The spirit of boisterousness and jollity fills this movement and makes for an entertaining finale to the concerto.

Bruch: Violin Concerto No. 1 in G minor

Max Bruch wrote his first violin concerto in 1866 (revised 1867). It is one of the most popular for the instrument being somewhat shorter than some others but still full of rich, lyrical melodies which suit the violin so well, as well as having plenty of scope for the soloist to impress.

Bruch writes for a conservative-sized orchestra: in addition to strings there are eight woodwind players (two each of flutes, oboes, clarinets and bassoons), four horns, two trumpets and timpani.

There are three movements, which is traditional for the concerto, but unusually the first is called *Vorspiel* or 'Prelude' and links directly into the slow movement.

First movement: Allegro moderato

We saw in Mozart's horn concerto the typical way a Classical period concerto starts: with a long orchestral introduction to set the scene. Increasingly, in the 19th century concerto, composers looked for a way of creating a dramatic start using the soloist.

Here Bruch has only five bars for the orchestra – two bars of a timpani rumble and then three bars of chords in the woodwinds – before the violinist is underway with an unaccompanied phrase that is played with a free sense of rhythm (*ad libitum*). It is a dramatic entry with the first note being the rich-sounding lowest note of the violin and then a rapid ascent using arpeggios. A second similar passage follows that takes the violin to the G three octaves above its starting note. This awakens the full orchestra into action and the main substance of the movement gets underway at figure A (bar 15).

The next violin entry shows considerable scope for using the instrument's various capabilities, combining:

■ Double- and then quadruple-stopping
■ Dazzling rapid arpeggio figuration across all four strings

- Lyrical writing in a falling phrase
- Final double-stopping in 6ths which sound sonorous and are comfortable to play.

Similarly the expressive second theme (after figure B) makes full use of the violin's wide compass as a sequence of trills soar high above the stave.

Much of the time the orchestra is quite restrained: it very much has a supporting role, offering a backdrop for the solo violin to be set against. Sometimes the woodwinds come to the fore briefly to provide some contrast of timbre.

Halfway through the movement the solo violin has a rising chromatic scale in semiquavers. This marks the start of an exciting passage in which the tempo accelerates (*stringendo*) and there is an irresistible build-up of intensity over 18 bars in which the soloist has non-stop virtuoso semiquavers. As this reaches a point of conclusion the orchestra swells thrillingly and launches into a lengthy passage without the soloist in which Bruch makes the most of the richness of tone and texture of the 19th-century Romantic orchestra.

When this eventually subsides the movement returns to the music of the opening to the concerto, which, after a short while, takes a change of direction to link with the slow movement.

Second movement: Adagio

The two movements are linked by a sustained B♭ in the orchestral violins: the minor 3rd of the key of the first movement, but now the 5th of the key of the slow movement, which is in E♭ major.

The soloist immediately presents the main theme of the movement over a velvet texture of sustained orchestral strings playing *pp*. The effect is one of rapt beauty.

This whole movement is full of long-breathed, expressive melodies that make for some exquisite music and goes a long way to explaining the wide popularity of this concerto. The first phrase illustrates well how Bruch achieves this through his melodic writing. The vast majority of the theme is built from conjunct steps, making the melody easily memorable and easy to sing, but every so often there

Note that Bruch indicates that the soloist should play most this theme on the D string and the final three bars on the G string. This adds to the lush quality of the tone, rather than playing the tune on slightly brighter-sounding higher strings.

is a wide interval: the rising 5th in bar 2, the falling 6th in bar 5, the rising 6th into bar 11. The rising leaps create a sense of yearning; falling leaps add poignancy and nostalgia:

After this initial statement of the theme, Bruch creates a very special texture in the accompaniment with discreetly rippling demisemiquavers in the second violins, pairs of pizzicato quavers in the bass, and long sustained harmony notes in the horns and violas.

The writing for the solo violin becomes increasingly elaborate, with some testing figuration to negotiate, but the music is only ever poetic. Twice Bruch visits the remote key of G♭ major (figure C and figure F) and this heightens the feeling of tenderness in the movement.

There is a short orchestral climax either side of figure H followed by a solo violin entry in the surprising key of C major. The music then subsides and returns to E♭ major for an ending of considerable poise and repose.

Third movement: Allegro energico

The finale starts with a cunning short introduction that begins with distant tremolo violas playing E♭ and G, notes that have been very significant in the previous slow movement in E♭ major. Very soon, however, the flats are dropped as the introduction moves towards a dominant pedal of G at bar 11 and its resolution is very definitely into bright G major rather than the brooding G minor of the first movement.

The main theme is played by the solo violin and is a very flamboyant affair with the melody mostly played in 3rds and use made of the lower two open strings – there is almost a dash of gypsy spirit here:

The soloist dominates the music for quite a while and then, at figure C, the main theme is played **ff** by the whole orchestra.

Some secondary material follows for a while but this efficiently builds up to figure E where a new and expansive theme is heard in D major, firstly in the orchestra and then on the violin, using its rich G-string tone:

The development section is rather brief and unremarkable after the glorious second subject. The recapitulation starts at figure G and follows a conventional course with the broad second subject now returning in the tonic of G major. The design is so efficient that Bruch does not give the soloist chance for a cadenza; instead there is a headlong dash for the end with the final scurrying bars marked Presto.

Listening ideas

If you want to explore this topic further there you may wish to explore some of the hundreds of concertos that have been written over the past 250 years. Among this rich repertoire are:

- Piano concertos: Brahms, Grieg and Ravel
- Violin concertos: Beethoven, Mendelssohn and Tchaikovsky
- Cello concertos: Dvořák, Saint-Saëns and Elgar
- Flute concerto: Nielsen
- Clarinet concertos: Weber and Copland
- Oboe concerto: Richard Strauss
- Saxophone concerto: Glazunov
- Trumpet concerto: Haydn
- Horn concerto: Richard Strauss
- Guitar concerto: Rodrigo.

You may like to listen to a concerto written for the instrument you play.

MUSIC FOR VOICES

Introduction

Singing is one of the most natural ways of making music and found the world over. This category of the specification is almost infinitely wide and potentially includes the following genres:

- Madrigal – an unaccompanied part song associated with the later Renaissance and early Baroque periods
- Opera – a staged drama in which the whole story is expressed through continuous music

- Mass – the setting of particular sections of the Catholic liturgy used in church services
- Oratorio – large-scale settings of stories to be performed in a concert, not in a theatre
- Song – settings of poetry for a solo singer usually accompanied by piano.

The diversity here is huge, but remember that you do not have to be learning a history of each genre; rather, AQA want to encourage you to explore and experience as much of this music as you can during your course so that you are used to responding analytically to what you hear.

Purcell: 'An Evening Hymn' from *Harmonia sacra* of 1688

Henry Purcell

Purcell (1659–1695) had only a short life, but in that time he showed himself to be a composer of great talent and originality. This solo song from the mid-Baroque period is one of the finest examples of Purcell's mastery of ground bass technique.

You will find the song published in various keys; for the current purposes we are using an edition in G major. There are recordings available of various different types of voice; look out for a recording of a countertenor singing the song: the song suits this kind of voice well and it is a great chance to get used to the difference between the sound of a male countertenor and female voice.

The accompaniment for the song is written for basso continuo (see page 66). In practice this means a cello playing the bass line and a harmony instrument, possibly organ, harpsichord or lute, to play chords based on the cello line and to fit the code of numbers under the stave.

The continuo plays a five-bar introduction. This comprises a rolling, conjunct melody in the bass:

Look through the score of the song, or listen carefully to a recording, and you will soon realise that this bass line melody repeats time and time again: in total it comes 22 times. This is known as the 'ground'.

In the middle of the song the ground is transposed, starting from B in bar 33, and from D for three repetitions from bar 39. Otherwise all other repetitions of the ground start from G.

Because the ground starts on the tonic and ends on the dominant, it can seem that the first note is actually the last note as a perfect cadence is heard. Purcell skilfully uses this slight ambiguity to create many places in the vocal line where the natural end of a phrase and start of the next do not dovetail with the ground.

The vocal line is mostly conjunct, but a few phrases are more disjunct to give contrast, especially the 'Dear God' line at bar 26 where the vocal phrase anticipates the start of the ground:

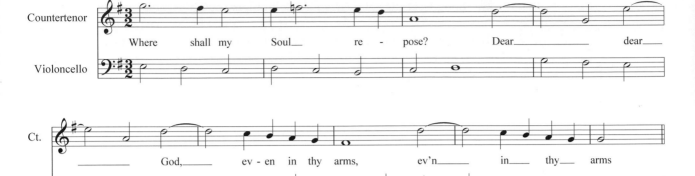

There is a very attractive evolving of mood through the course of the song. There is an intimacy to the first third and real tranquillity midway with the long, seven-beat note on 'rest'. In the second half, however, there is a more fervent energy, derived from the use of dotted rhythms and having many notes for certain words (e.g. 'sing' and 'hallelujah'): a technique known as **melisma**.

Haydn: 'The Heavens Are Telling' from *The Creation*

After many decades working as a court composer, Haydn had the chance to travel to England in the 1790s. Here he heard performances of Handel's oratorios and resolved to write something similar. The result was *The Creation* which he completed in 1798. Some consider it to be his masterpiece.

The oratorio tells the story of God's creation of the world as found in the book of Genesis in the Bible. This popular choral movement, which is often performed separately by choirs, comes at the end of Part I of the oratorio. The movement is in C major which allows for trumpets in the orchestra. The brisk tempo and upbeat to each phrase helps to create music of celebratory good cheer.

The chorus comes in six sections:

1–18	18–38	38–48	49–95	95–109	110–end
Choral section – homophonic	Solo trio section	Choral section parts used in pairs	Solo trio section	Choral section parts used in pairs again	Contrapuntal choral section

The melodic ideas are immediately appealing, especially the second choral phrase which is all conjunct:

A similar phrase is the basis of the contrapuntal final section of the movement.

Listen out for the following features:

One good recording of *The Creation* is conducted by Eugen Jochum on Philips, ASIN B000041C1.

- The simple tonic and dominant harmony in the first section
- The touches of C minor – see the flats – for mention of the night in the second section
- The tenors and basses entering a bar before the sopranos and altos in the third section
- The colourful use of the woodwinds in accompanying the fourth section
- The building of tension over the eight bars of a dominant pedal in the final section (bars 159–166)
- The simple tonic and dominant chords in the orchestra to finish the movement.

Notice also that throughout the setting of the words rarely gives more than one note for each syllable. There are none of the long melismas that we found in the Purcell 'Evening Hymn'. This style of setting words is known as **syllabic**.

Puccini: 'O mio babbino caro' from *Gianni Schicchi*

Puccini is one of the great operatic composers of Italian music. *Gianni Schicchi* is the third in a trio of one-act operas collectively known as *Il Trittico*, and received its first performance in 1918.

This famous aria 'O mio babbino caro' ('O my beloved daddy') from the opera is sung by Lauretta (a part for a soprano singer) to her father. She wants to marry her beloved Rinuccio and is pleading for her father's blessing.

The mood is perfectly captured in Puccini's melody. The opening two-bar phrase generally falls in a submissive fashion, but the octave leap in the next phrase reaches out in a heartfelt fashion. This leap is often sung by opera singers with noticeable portamento (see page 57): listen out carefully to see if this is done in your recording.

The phrase structure sees a brief move to the dominant at bar 8 and then a return to the opening melody before a different direction is taken after four bars. The ending is very tender with the accompaniment reduced to a minimum.

The orchestration is sumptuous with the violins doubling the melody at the upper octave and a harp discreetly rippling in the middle of the texture.

Listening ideas

There are huge areas of repertoire relevant to this topic that you may wish to explore further. Works by the following composers would be a good place to start:

- Songs: Schubert, Brahms, Fauré
- Oratorio: Handel, Elgar
- Opera: Mozart, Rossini, Richard Strauss.

CHAMBER MUSIC

Introduction

'Chamber music' describes music that is intended to be played by a small group of musicians, quite possibly in a semi-private manner, such as at home.

Chamber music became a major part of composers' output in the Classical period following the establishment of the string quartet (attributed to Haydn principally), and grew in popularity as the increasing affluence of the middle class meant that there was more leisure time for educated people. Soon all manner of trios, quartets, quintets and sextets were being written.

Most of these works follow a similar four-movement plan to the symphony; indeed they are almost like symphonies in a more intimate guise.

© www.shutterstock.com

Common groupings

By far the most common group found in chamber music from the early Classical period onwards is the string quartet comprising two violins, one viola and one cello (as shown in the picture on the previous page). Other regular formations include:

- Piano trio: violins, cello and piano
- String trio: violin, viola, cello
- String quintet: two violins, one viola and two cellos (e.g. Schubert), *or* two violins, two violas and one cello (e.g. Mozart)
- Piano quartet: piano, violin, viola and cello
- Piano quintet: piano plus string quartet
- Clarinet quintet: clarinet plus string quartet
- String sextet: two violins, two violas and two cellos.

Mozart: String quintet in C major, K. 515

Mozart learned to write string quartets from the example of the older Haydn. There are accounts of them playing quartets together in Vienna. However, the string quintet was Mozart's own innovation. He played the viola, so it is, perhaps, no surprise that he chose to add an extra viola to the quartet to form his quintet. He wrote five string quintets in all; the C major one was written in 1787.

There are four movements:

1. Allegro
2. Menuetto
3. Andante
4. Allegro.

First movement: Allegro

This lengthy movement of 368 bars follows the standard three-part structure of sonata form:

1–151	152–208	209–368
Exposition	Development	Recapitulation

The opening is an archetypal Classical period passage in many ways:

- The melodic shapes in the cello are all arpeggios
- The phrases in the first violin include a turn – a very Classical ornament
- The first phrase in bars 1–5 moves from chord I to chord V
- The answering phrase moves back from chord V to chord I
- The opening paragraph ends with an imperfect cadence in bar 119.

Here is the opening five bars:

There are some points of originality, however:

- The opening phrases are each five bars long, rather than the usual four
- The texture creates antiphony between first violin and cello whilst the inner parts provide the harmony
- After the general pause bar in bar 20, there's a re-statement of the opening with the texture reversed and in C minor.

A little further on, Mozart becomes very resourceful with his harmonic vocabulary, finding a way to use many flats around bar 48, and many sharps from bar 62. From bar 76 there is a sequence of five entries feature the turn pattern rising up through the texture.

The second subject at bar 86 is an elegant flowing line of quavers in the first violin over a tonic pedal (now in G major). Another lengthy tonic pedal marks the start of a codetta passage at bar 131.

The development opens with a distorted version of the quintet's opening with the inner parts once more playing repeating quavers. From bar 171, however, there is greater contrapuntal writing with independent lines in all five instruments.

Second movement: Menuetto

Unusually the Menuet is used as the second movement in this quintet. The opening phrase is played by both violins, which are a third apart: the ideal interval for creating attractive consonant harmony. In the second half of the Menuet this idea is pursued further with various combinations of pairs of instruments used in this way, a 3rd apart. In bars 35–36 the violins are a 3rd apart with an arch-shaped phrase; meanwhile the violas are a 3rd apart with a mirror image (inversion) of the violins' phrase.

The Trio is in the subdominant key of F major, and is in binary form with a modulation to the C at the halfway point. Listen out for how both halves of the Trio end with similar material, just in different keys. The start of the trio also reappears in the second half.

The Menuet is played again after the trio to form an overall ternary structure.

Third movement: Andante

The Andante is an exquisitely ornate movement in F major. One of its most notable features is the writing for the first viola, which is often in a starring role. This was the part that Mozart himself would have played.

There is a lot of ornamentation here with many turns and plenty of florid melodic writing, often with touches of chromaticism. At the end of the first half of the movement (bars 55–56) there is a substantial perfect cadence in the movement's dominant, which involves lengthy trills in the top three parts and an arpeggio in the cello.

Fourth movement: Allegro

The quintet ends with a light-hearted and skittish rondo movement in duple time. The main rondo theme is stated immediately at the start by the first violin and is built out of two-bar units. This is treated to a diatonic harmonisation with plenty of energy derived from the use of quaver rest in the inner parts.

A feature of this finale is how often the first violin plays alone without support from the other four players. The final phrase of the quintet involves all five players in octaves and is a descending broken chord figure based on a C major triad. It seems to bring the whole work full circle and balances the rising C major arpeggio with which the work started;

Mendelssohn: Piano Trio No. 1 in D minor Op. 49

Felix Mendelssohn

Mendelssohn wrote his first piano trio in 1839. It is a large-scale work which shows a fascinating blend between Classical and Romantic traits. Above all it has some fine piano writing which shows the developments in the instrument that had occurred since the start of the 19th century.

There are four movements:

1. Molto allegro e agitato

2. Andante con moto tranquillo

3. Scherzo – Leggiero e vivace

4. Finale – Allegro assai appassionato.

First movement: Molto allegro ed agitato

There is a distant opening with the theme heard in the cello against a softly pulsating piano accompaniment in which the left hand plays on the beat, but the right hand is off the beat. The theme grows in confidence, with the violin taking it over after 16 bars. From this point try to listen to the rising bass line in the cello and piano left hand as the music reaches f for the first time.

Molto allegro ed agitato

The piano soon becomes very busy with rapid triplet quavers in the right hand, and, at figure B, the main first theme in octaves in the left hand. There is a sense of the music surging forwards at times in a brooding manner, and the use of sf markings places this very much in the Romantic era. However, the next new theme, heard in the cello after figure C, has a very classical sense of proportion with four four-bar phrases:

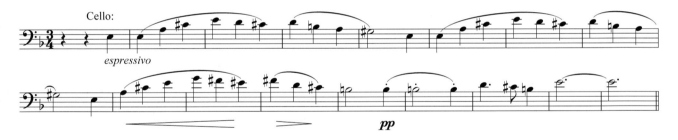

There is an extensive development section, which once again points to Romantic traits with a variety of moods. The point of recapitulation is striking, because although the cello and piano play similar music to the start of the exposition, the violin (which was not involved at the start) now plays a new countermelody.

The coda to the movement is somewhat fast and has a stunningly virtuoso part for the pianist with cascading triplet quavers scurrying away until the end of the movement.

Second movement: Andante con moto tranquillo

The trio moves to B♭ major for this tender slow movement, which is reminiscent of some of Mendelssohn's *Songs without Words* for solo piano.

Listen to the opening piano statement of the theme and chart where the high notes of the phrase come: at first they rise – D, then F, then G – but then they are in reverse order as the eight-bar phrase comes to rest on an imperfect cadence:

At this point the strings enter with the melody for the answering phrase and the piano takes a step back to having an accompanimental role.

There is greater passion in the central section of the movement when the music moves to B♭ minor and triplet quaver rhythms appear in the piano part. When the main theme returns after figure V, the textures are quite lavish and skilfully handled.

Third movement: Scherzo. Leggiero e vivace

As a pianist, Mendelssohn was renowned for his staccato playing. This skill is very much required by all three players in this movement which speed along in a sparkling manner. There are various other tricks adding to the fun, such as the hemiola cross-rhythm in the piano part just before the strings join in, and the rapid-fire antiphony between strings and piano in bars 13–15.

Again the pianist has some tricky passages to negotiate, such as the double octaves (i.e. octaves in both hands simultaneously), followed by lightening fast arpeggios, going into figure Dd.

There is little opportunity to catch breath in the movement which evaporates into thin air in a dainty conclusion.

Fourth movement: Finale. Allegro assai appassionata

The finale to the Trio has many contrasting ideas competing for the listener's attention:

- The regular rhythmic tread of the opening theme on the piano
- The secondary material over a flamboyant broken chord figuration in the piano
- A broad, lyrical melody in the cello after figure Nn, somewhat in the manner of a *Song without Words*
- A middle section to this more lyrical passage, which is heard on the piano
- A glittering coda from figure Xx with more double octaves in the piano.

The movement as a whole is a hugely enjoyable showpiece for the piano trio genre, and the appearance of the broad, lyrical theme finally in the tonic major (D major) is a moment of significant culmination.

 Listening ideas

The 19th century, especially, was a time when many wonderful chamber works were composed and there are many riches to explore in this area. Some key works include:

- Mozart: Clarinet quintet
- Beethoven: String quartets
- Brahms: String sextets
- Schumann: Piano quartet
- Dvořák: Piano trios
- Elgar: Piano quintet.

THE SONATA

Introduction

The word 'sonata' has been used to describe a variety of pieces, but since the Classical period it has been used to denote a major work for a solo instrumentalist, possibly with piano accompaniment. Sonatas usually have three movements, though four is not uncommon.

Mozart: Piano Sonata in C major, K. 309

The sonata really came of age during the Classical period in the hands of Haydn and Mozart. This C major sonata was written in the autumn of 1777, and is one of the earliest of Mozart's sonatas for piano. There are, as was usual in Classical sonatas, three movements:

- Allegro con spirito
- Andante un poco adagio
- Allegretto grazioso.

First movement: Allegro con spirito

This movement provides a very clear example of one of the most important structures in music: sonata form. In total there are 155 bars, and it should be easy to both hear and see from the music where the main subdivisions fall:

Bars 1–58	Bars 59–93	Bars 94–155
Exposition	Development	Recapitulation

The exposition presents two main sections, which are known as the first subject and second subject. The first subject opens with a very strong idea based on a C major triad. In all there are three phrases or musical sentences in the first subject and, unusually, these break free from the obvious two, four or eight-bar units, being seven, seven and six bars respectively. Here is the first of these phrases (or sentences):

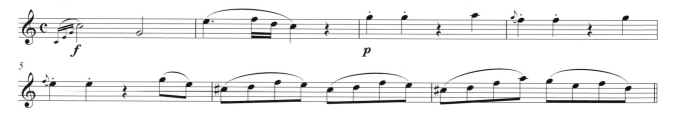

A passage of 12 bars follows which has the function of modulating to G major: the dominant key. This is known as the transition.

The second subject presents a very different, more delicate melody which is played in the new key of G major – look out for the F sharps. It starts like this:

The second subject with a very strong perfect cadence, emphasised by a bar-long trill in the melody (bars 53–54). There are then five bars to round off the exposition; these are known as the codetta.

The development provides an opportunity to explore the potential of the musical ideas presented in the exposition, while passing through some keys that are more remote from our starting key of C major. In this movement, Mozart concentrates on the main first subject idea during the development: you will hear the triad-shaped tune played in G minor at bar 59, D minor at bar 67, and A minor at bar 86. The rhythm of this idea is also used in other bars with a somewhat different melodic contour. From bar 82 Mozart also uses material from the short codetta that we heard at the end of the exposition.

Notice how, in bars 90–93, the development finishes with a version of the first subject that emphasises a G major triad plus an F natural. This is a typical way of preparing for the return of the tonic key (C major) which we expect at the start of the recapitulation.

In many ways the recapitulation follows the same plan as the exposition, but there are a few important differences:

  ■ The second phrase (or musical sentence) of the first subject is, surprisingly, played in C minor rather than C major

- The transition (from bar 116) is altered so that it ends with a G major arpeggio and not a D major arpeggio; this means the music is not going to modulate at this point like it did in the exposition
- The second subject is now in the tonic key (C major) rather than the dominant (G major) and the theme is first heard in the left hand rather than the right hand
- The codetta is now 8 bars long instead of 5 in order to provide a more substantial ending to the movement as a whole (Mozart actually uses the main motif of the first subject to achieve this).

Second and third movements

The other two movements provide contrast and a sense of balance to the sonata as a whole. There is a very elegant and expressive slow movement, which is in the subdominant key of F major. The opening graceful theme is immediately repeated at bar 17 and then returns twice more (bars 45 and 65), each time being more and more decorated, so that at its final appearance the tune is encased in swirls of demisemiquavers. A secondary theme in C major is first heard at bar 33, and this too returns in an ornately decorated version at bar 53.

For the final movement the sonata returns to C major. Like the final movement of Mozart's Horn Concerto we looked at earlier, this finale is also in Rondo form (see page 78). The main Rondo theme is heard immediately as the movement starts and subsequently returns at bars 93 and 189. It is also used for the short and subdued codetta with which the movement, and indeed the whole sonata, ends.

Beethoven: Piano Sonata in C♯ minor, 'Moonlight'

Beethoven's 32 piano sonatas are held in high esteem by pianists. None is more well-known than this, the 'Moonlight'. Beethoven wrote it in 1801 when he was on the brink of the new Romantic age in music. Certainly, there are some innovative aspects to the sonata, not least starting with a slow movement. However, it is highly unlikely that Beethoven was responsible for the work's nickname; instead, he called it 'Sonata quasi una fantasia'.

There are three movements:

1. Adagio sostenuto

2. Allegretto

3. Presto agitato.

Ludwig van Beethoven

First movement: Adagio sostenuto

With this opening movement Beethoven found a new way to begin a sonata, so instead of the customary Allegro in sonata form, the sonata opens with a soft, haunting Adagio.

This whole movement is characterised by the slowly rippling triplet quaver arpeggios over slowly moving octaves in the bass. There is a beauty to this texture, but the minor tonality also makes the mood quite frozen. The melody enters from bar 6 and is of little distinct interest, with its first six notes all being G# and the whole phrase fitting a narrow range of pitch. Nonetheless, it adds to the sense of poise in the music.

In the central section (from bar 32), the triplets once more come to the fore until the melody returns in bar 43. Listen out carefully for bar 57: the only bar in the whole movement that has the harmony changing on every beat. This quicker harmonic rhythm is very telling.

At the end of the movement the music sinks into the bass register before the final C# minor chords.

Second movement: Allegretto

This movement looks as though it is in a completely unrelated key: five flats after four sharps, but, in fact, both movements have the same tonic note: the note that can variously be called C# or Db. The first movement is in C# minor; this is in Db major.

The movement is essentially like a Menuet and Trio: the Allegretto is played again (because of the *da capo* instruction) after the Trio. After the gently rippling texture of the first movement, this one is more strictly homophonic. In the Trio the melody in the right hand is in octaves in a mid-to-low register, which is quite a curious device.

Third movement: Presto agitato

The Finale of the sonata is a spectacular movement that is full of energy. The tempo is very fast indeed, and the feature of **sf** chords coming on the fourth beat of many bars makes a big impact. The opening semiquaver figuration in the right hand uses broken chords:

When a more lyrical melodic strand is introduced in the right hand (bar 21) the agitated semiquavers are still rumbling away in the left hand. The other contrasting material is the homophonic quaver chords first heard at bar 43.

Listening ideas

There is a very wide range of sonatas for most instruments that you could investigate for this topic. The following are highly recommended for you to listen to:

- Piano: Liszt – Sonata in B minor; Ravel – Sonatine
- Violin: Brahms – Sonata in G major; Elgar – Sonata in E minor
- Cello: Rachmaninov
- Flute: Poulenc
- Oboe: Saint-Saëns
- Clarinet: Brahms – Sonata in E♭.

POPULAR MUSIC OF THE 20TH AND 21ST CENTURIES

It can be tempting to think that pop music was invented in the 20th century, and that before then there was only classical music. This, however, is not a true picture: there has always been popular music. In the Medieval era there are accounts of minstrels and love songs that provided a very different role for music than the serious music that was used in the monasteries and cathedrals of Europe.

Where the 20th century changed the balance was in the development of recording. In Medieval days, the minstrels' music was often only preserved insofar as one generation passed their music onto the next aurally, while music of the church would be preserved by monks in beautiful illuminated manuscripts. Furthermore, of course, you would only hear the music played by your local minstrels.

With the rise of recording, popular music has a means to be broadcast around the world almost instantaneously from the moment of its creation, and the popular musical styles of previous generations continue to be aired. These days there are radio stations specialising in just about every style of popular music from the last 100 years. The film and computer game industries have generated other areas of music for mass consumption.

From this century of popular music, AQA have selected five areas which you need to study for your GCSE exam:

- Blues
- Popular Music of the 1960s
- Rock Music, R'n'B, Hip hop
- Music Theatre
- Film Music.

Within these five areas it is up to you and your teacher to select works to study: there are no compulsory songs set by AQA. It is helpful for you to learn the main features of the styles so that you can comment on how elements of music are being used.

BLUES

Listening ideas

A useful compilation double CD set for this topic is *The very best of the Blues* (Nascente NSCDD2005).

The Blues originated among the black people of America in the first half of the 20th century, and flourished in the southern states where the slave trade had taken many black people of African origin.

The blues incorporated various African elements such as the use of call-and-response, and the style of melody common in the black people's spiritual tradition. It became one of the most important influences on popular music throughout the western world as the century progressed. Common features of the blues include:

- A 12-bar structure to the verse
- Melodic lines using flattened notes (usually the 3rd, 5th and 7th)
- A growling timbre used in the singing (sometimes imitated in saxophone or trumpet playing too)
- Lyrics expressing the hardships of life for the African-American community.

'Boom, Boom' – John Lee Hooker

One of the earliest types of Blues music was known as 'Delta Blues', the delta in question being that of the River Mississippi.

John Lee Hooker was born in Mississippi, home of the Blues, in 1917 and was one of the most important blues musicians after the Second World War. 'Boom, Boom' was recorded in late 1961 and released the next year.

The song is built around the 12-bar blues pattern, which is one of the most important elements of the Blues style. These verses are constructed out of three four-bar phrases, and a set chord progression (with a few possible variants – given in brackets) as follows:

Bar	1	2	3	4	5	6	7	8	9	10	11	12
Chord	I	I (IV)	I	I	IV	IV	I	I	V	V (IV)	I	I

John Lee Hooker

This pattern is present from the start in the opening instrumental 12 bars in which the guitar plays solo in the odd-numbered bars and the band joins in for the even-numbered bars (piano, bass and drums in particular). The chord pattern is as in the chart on the previous page, avoiding the options in brackets on this occasion.

Listen carefully to the piano playing: the chord is played in a broken figuration, largely in quavers which are played in the 'swing' style. This creates a 'boogie-woogie' effect – something which John Lee Hooker incorporated into his take on the Blues.

At the end of the 12-bar intro, the voice (Hooker) enters and there are two verses, each of which play through the 12-bar chord pattern again with the voice now taking the role that the guitar took in the intro – i.e., singing solo in the odd-numbered bars. A third vocal verse starts, but the vocals give way to a slightly more free and extended instrumental passage. Listen out for the growl of the tenor and baritone saxophones here that were part of Hooker's band.

After a while Hooker's vocals re-enter, now so gravel-like in timbre that it is virtually speech rather than singing. The song soon comes to its close as it fades out.

'Looking for Somebody' – Fleetwood Mac

The band Fleetwood Mac was formed in London in 1967; their debut album, which included this song, was released the following year and was one of the most successful of the time, staying in the charts for nine months.

Here again, the 12-bar blues pattern is used, and there is an instrumental intro. There are, however, some important differences from the previous song:

- Instead of the solo guitar, there is a harmonica (or mouth organ) used as the melodic instrument; its wailing tone is well-suited to the blues style
- The chord progression this time makes use of the option for chord IV in the 10th bar: listen out carefully for this
- The bass line has a sense of riff that includes straight quavers on the upbeat, starting on the flattened (or 'blue') 3rd, and a syncopated rhythm emphasising the offbeat after the second beat of the bar.

Listen out, too, for the straight quavers (or eighths) played on the ride cymbal in the drums.

When the voice enters, there is a 16-bar verse, created by repeating the first four-bar phrase (over a static chord I). Two such verses lead to a new instrumental section for the solo harmonica which reverts to the 12-bar pattern.

The coda, or 'outro' features an off-beat repetitive tonic note in the harmonica, and the music gradually fades out.

POPULAR MUSIC OF THE 1960S

The 1960s have a famous reputation for being a decade of free spirit and excess. The years of austerity following the Second World War were finally forgotten as a new generation (the baby boomers) came to their independence. Their fashion, music and values shaped the decade.

'Penny Lane' – The Beatles

The Beatles

The Beatles are one of the most successful bands of all times, enjoying phenomenal success both sides of the Atlantic. Formed in Liverpool in 1960, they broke up in 1970: the Beatles are *the* iconic 60s band. They were a four-piece band:

- John Lennon – rhythm guitar and vocals
- Paul McCartney – bass guitar and vocals
- George Harrison – lead guitar and vocals
- Ringo Starr – drums and vocals.

Penny Lane was first released early in 1967 and is named after a street in the band's home city of Liverpool. The song, primarily composed by McCartney, actually only reached number two in the charts, but the band's producer, George Martin, thought that the song (which was paired with Lennon's 'Strawberry Fields Forever') was the band's best-ever single release.

The song is structured in a simple verse-chorus pattern in which the verse is played twice before each chorus. There is no intro or outro. Unusually, the verses are in B major and the choruses in A major. This change of key is handled with great skill (a move to B minor near the end of the verse eases the move into the chorus; a twist in the chord sequence at the end of the chorus moves towards the dominant of B major for the start of the next verse); it also underlines the change in the lyrics: the verses are written in the third person, whereas the chorus is in the first person.

The song is renowned for its instrumental section: the second half of the second verse has no vocals, instead there is a trumpet solo played on the small piccolo trumpet played by David Mason. The idea for this came from a performance of Bach's *Brandenburg* Concerto which this classical trumpeter had presented on BBC television. The bright, ringing timbre of this instrument provides a very memorable interlude in the song. Listen out for the rhythm at the start of the solo: two semiquavers leading to a quaver on the downbeat, and then this rhythmic cell is re-used; a similar rhythm is found at the start of the *Brandenburg* Concerto.

After the third chorus, the music returns to B major, but the chorus is now played again in the higher key, and the piccolo trumpet returns. The song ends without any prolongation after this final chorus passage.

The full structure of the song, then, is as follows:

Verse part 1	B major	Vocals
Verse part 2	B major	Vocals
Chorus	A major	Vocals
Verse part 1	B major	Vocals
Verse part 2	B major	Instrumental – trumpet solo
Chorus	A major	Vocals
Verse part 1	B major	Vocals
Verse part 2	B major	Vocals
Chorus	A major	Vocals
Chorus	B major	Vocals with trumpet

Listen out carefully for the bass line and see if you can hear the difference between how the bass moves in the verse and in the chorus. In the verse it has a largely stepwise falling pattern; in the chorus it moves upwards (A – C♯ – D).

Also have a listen for the drum patterns which usually emphasise the second and fourth beats of the bar (the backbeats). Just before the instrumental solo, mention of the fireman is coloured with a fireman's bell.

ROCK MUSIC, R'n'B, HIP HOP

These three styles cover many areas of popular music of the last 40 years. Rock is a very broad field with many sub-categories such as glam rock, heavy metal, stadium rock, progressive rock and punk rock. Common traits are a dependence on electric guitars (with heavily strummed chords and often using effects such as distortion), a heavy marking of the pulse in the rhythm section (sometimes just the backbeats, sometimes all four beats of the bar), simple harmonic progressions and catchy melodic shapes.

R'n'B (Rhythm and Blues) is a term first used in the late 1940s to describe some African American popular music. In more contemporary times it is used to describe a type of soul- and funk-influenced pop music produced by artists such as Rihanna, Beyoncé, Mariah Carey, Alicia Keys and Craig David. Contemporary R'n'B tends to have a smooth vocal style, often making use of melisma (the use of several notes to one syllable or vowel sound), rhythms created by drum machines, some guitar riffs to give a sense of rock style, or perhaps a saxophone solo to bring a jazz influence.

For more on melisma see page 84.

Hip hop has its origins in the 1970s when it was a movement in the Bronx in New York City. It involves the vocal technique of rapping: speaking rhythmically, and often in rhyme, to a beat. The beat can be generated by a DJ using turntables or produced using sampling of other material. Sometimes this involves drum machines and synthesisers. In the last decade or so the style has diversified as it has fused with other popular styles, for instance, Puerto Rican singer Lisa M has mixed hip hop with merengue (see page 116) to create merenrap (sometimes called merenhouse), while a fusion with soul has led to nu soul (or neo soul).

'Whatever you want' – Status Quo

Status Quo is an English rock band whose origins go back to the early 1960s. The name Status Quo became established in 1967 and since then they have been one of the most successful bands in rock music, producing over 60 chart hits in the UK, 22 of which have reached the top 10. Over the decades there have been changes of personnel, but founder members Francis Rossi (lead guitar) and Rick Parfitt (rhythm guitar) still head up the band.

'Whatever you want' was written by Parfitt and Andy Bown (keyboards) and was released in 1979 and reached number four in the UK charts.

The song opens with a quiet and mellow guitar solo. There then follows a driving rhythm on the rhythm guitar on an open 5th of D and A (sometimes referred to as a power chord). This lasts for eight bars (listen for the extra C natural played on the lead guitar on the fourth beat of each bar), with a crescendo throughout this time, and creates a growing sense of anticipation. This finds resolution when the music moves into D major for the main material of the song.

© Getty Images

Status Quo

The song uses a simple eight-bar pattern as follows.

'A' section chord sequence:

Bar	1	2	3	4	5	6	7	8
Chord	I (D)	I	I	I	V (A)	V	I	I

This pattern is played twice by guitars, with the drums entering on the second time. The effect of this drum entry is to continue the sense of mounting excitement, until finally the vocals start.

There is a contrasting 'middle 8' in which the chord changes more frequently and uses some more colourful chords some of which do not usually occur in D major.

'B' section chord sequence:

Bar	1	2	3	4	5	6	7	8
Chord	F	C	D	D	F	C→B	E	A

Listen carefully for the strong effect when beats 2 and 4 of the third bar and beat 2 of the fourth bar are accented with guitar chords, thereby creating a kick to the rhythm at this point.

These two eight-bar units comprise the whole song, but for a few details. The full structure of the song is as follows:

Intro part 1	Guitar solo
Intro part 2	Eight bars of driving power chord of D
'A' section	Guitars only
'A' section	Guitars and drums
'A' section	Vocals enter
'A' section	Vocals
'B' section ('middle 8')	With vocals
'A' section	With vocals
Instrumental – lead guitar solo	Based on 'B' section but with some differences
'A' section	With vocals
'B' section	With vocals
'A' section but with short extension	With vocals
'A' section	Guitars and drums
'A' section	Guitars and drums
'A' section with short extension	Guitars and drums

Listen out for the way the song ends: two bars before the end the music has a dominant chord (A), and the return to the final tonic chord (D) is achieved through ascending semitones, creating a section of chromatic scale.

'Fallin'' – Alicia Keys

Alicia Keys was born in New York in 1981. She enjoyed and learned classical piano as a young girl before enrolling in performing arts school in Manhattan when she was 12. Her first album, *Songs in A Minor,* (in fact only one of the songs on the album is in A minor) was released in 2001; 'Fallin'' is the single taken from that album and reached number one in the American charts.

Alicia Keys

There is a hypnotic quality to the song that creates a sense of poignancy in the music. This is due to a number of factors:

- The tempo is slow – about 60 beats per minute (in $\frac{6}{8}$ time)
- The chord pattern is wholly dependent on two alternating chords
- Both chords are minor: Em and Bm⁷ – this creates a modal quality to the music with D naturals in E minor
- The piano figuration is based on rocking quaver arpeggio pattern, up and down creating an arch shape to each bar.

Listen out for the way the song starts: Keys sings 'I keep on falling in love' as an unaccompanied first line. What is noticeable is the flourish of notes on the word 'in'. This technique, called melisma, is typical of the R'n'B style.

With so many elements of the song having no variety (tempo, rhythm, key, chord pattern, etc.) the music could become very monotonous, but there are some details which add just enough change to keep the song sounding fresh. Among these are:

- Occasional bars without the piano arpeggio figuration
- The layering of the vocal tracks, including backing singers that add a hint of gospel style
- The varied drum patterns programmed by Kerry 'Krucial' Brothers
- The use of backing strings and the closing violin solo played by the Israeli Miri Ben-Ari
- A couple of bass runs in the piano from B down to the tonic E.

'My President is Black' – Young Jeezy

Young Jeezy is an American rapper born in 1977 in South Carolina. 'My President is Black' was first recorded on the morning that Barack Obama won the Democratic nomination for the presidential election in 2008, and is the final track of Jeezy's album *The Recession*. The lyrics contrast various colours, and also pay tribute to other figures in the black Civil Rights movement in America (Rosa Parks and Martin Luther King).

In the run-up to President Obama's inauguration in January 2009, a remix version was made in which Young Jeezy was joined by Jay-Z, an American hip hop artist and businessman (married to the singer Beyoncé). This was first performed in a nightclub in Washington DC, a couple of nights before the inauguration ceremony. This version is easy to find on YouTube.

The main musical substance on the backing beat is the strings which move five steps up the D major scale and then back again, with the upper and lower parts a 10th apart (starting from D and F♯). The music is in a steady $\frac{4}{4}$ and these string parts move in a dotted minim + crotchet pattern each bar.

Listen out for the other detail of the backing beat: the digitalised drum patterns, some extra string layers on top of the basic pattern, and some pulsating of the chords in crotchets after the 1' mark. The overall effect has a positive anthem-like message as the African-American community celebrates the landmark moment of the first black President of the USA.

© Getty Images

Young Jeezy

The history of musical plays, or 'musicals', as they are now known, goes back to the 19th century. By the 1920s, a decade of great exuberance and spirit in western society, they had become an immensely popular form of entertainment, especially in New York. The 1940s and 1950s are often regarded as the golden age of the musical, and many were made into highly successful film versions in this era. However, from Broadway in New York to the West End of London, musicals have continued to be a strong tradition in the theatre.

Among the major figures that have made a lasting impact on the musical in the last 100 years are:

- Richard Rodgers – *Oklahoma!* (1943), *The King and I* (1951), *The Sound of Music* (1959)
- Leonard Bernstein – *On the Town* (1944), *West Side Story* (1957)
- Stephen Sondheim – *A Little Night Music* (1973), *Sweeney Todd* (1979), *Into the Woods* (1986)
- Andrew Lloyd Webber – *Evita* (1978), *Phantom of the Opera* (1986), *The Woman in White* (2004)
- Claude-Michel Schönberg – *Les Misérables* (1980), *Miss Saigon* (1989), *Martin Guerre* (1996).

'Edelweiss' from *The Sound of Music* – Richard Rodgers

The Sound of Music is an account, based on real life, of a family of musical children, the von Trapps, who fled from Nazi Germany when their father, an Austrian, was ordered to join the German navy. A highly successful film version (it won 5 Oscars) was released in 1965.

'Edelweiss' is sung by the father, a widower, as his heart, frozen by his bereavement, melts and he rediscovers his love for his children and for music. The song is named after a white flower that grows high in the Alps and is a symbol of Austrian life continuing despite the Nazi occupation. It is a gentle, lyrical song in triple time and in B♭ major.

This well-known song is an excellent opportunity to study and understand the 32-bar song form. This is, by far, the most common form for composers to use when writing songs for musicals.

The 32 bars fall into four eight-bar phrases. Of these, the first, second and fourth share identical or similar melodies; the third phrase offers something contrasting. Listen carefully to this song and you will hear that the second and fourth phrases in this instance are identical melodies; the first phrase is very similar, but is a little different at the end. The reason is that the first phrase ends with an imperfect cadence, whereas the second and fourth phrases end with perfect cadences.

Clearly the lyricist (Oscar Hammerstein II) had this form in mind, because there are more syllables in the third quarter of the verse, and this allows for a slightly busier rhythm in the third phrase as well as other musical differences: a contrasting melodic shape, and a small modulation to the dominant created by the E♮ in the bass line.

The song's overall structure can be represented by the following chart:

Phrase	Lyrics	Melody
1	*Edelweiss, Edelweiss, Ev'ry morning you greet me*	'A'; imperfect cadence
2	*Small and white, Clean and bright, You look happy to meet me*	'A'; perfect cadence
3	*Blossom of snow may you bloom and grown, Bloom and grow for ever*	'B'; brief modulation to V
4	*Edelweiss, Edelweiss, bless my homeland for ever*	'A'; perfect cadence

In the film the Captain accompanies himself on the guitar, but listen out for how there is a very soft string backing that joins in after the first phrase adding to the nostalgic atmosphere of the song.

'Luck be a Lady' from *Guys and Dolls* – Frank Loesser

Guys and Dolls tells of a love story between Sky Masterson, a gambler, and Sarah Brown, a member of a Salvation Army style mission. In order to prove his love for Sarah, Sky has to persuade his fellow gamblers to attend the mission, something he can only do by making a bet over the roll of the dice. At the point this song occurs, he begs for 'Lady Luck' to be on his side.

© Getty Images

A production of *Guys and Dolls*

There is an introduction to the song in a fairly free rhythm with lots of words. Listen out for the rising scales on 'very unladylike way' and 'evening is over you might'. The chords through this section are quite spicy and include various blue notes.

The main melody of the song falls into the same AABA form as 'Edelweiss' although there are some significant differences:

- The phrases are not each eight bars long
- The second phrase is in a key a semitone higher than the first
- The third phrase is another semitone higher before the original key (C major) is resumed for the final phrase
- There continues to be blue notes, such as the flattened 7th on 'to-night' in the opening phrase.

The basic structure of the song is as follows:

Phrase	Melodic idea	Opening lyric of phrase	No. of bars	Key
1	A	*Luck be a lady tonight*	18	C
2	A	*Luck let a gentleman see*	18	D♭
3	B	*A lady doesn't leave her escort*	16	D
4	A	*So let's keep the party polite*	25	C

In spite of the number of bars used here, this form is still often known as 32-bar song form, or AABA form.

Listen out for the detail in the orchestral writing which gives this song, which is so pivotal to Sky's chances of getting his girl, an edge of excitement and tension. This includes:

- The continuous, fast 'um-cha' rhythm underpinning the song which is like an excited heartbeat
- Rapid flourishes in the woodwinds
- Brash, snarling interjections in the trombones and trumpets
- Fast, scurrying violins.

A famous film version of *Guys and Dolls* was made in 1955 starring Marlon Brando. Note that this has the song at a lower pitch (in A major rather than C major).

FILM MUSIC

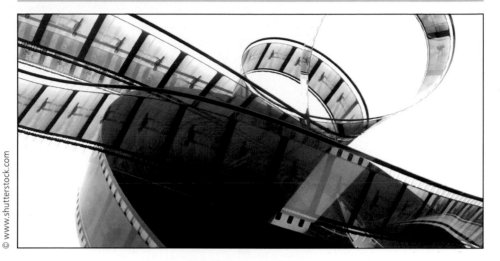

© www.shutterstock.com

Writing music for films and the cinema was the most significant new area of activity for composers of the 20th century. During the era of silent films music, usually played live in the cinema by an orchestra, or possiby an organist, was essential; after the development of synchronised sound in film (first achieved in *The Jazz Singer* in 1927), it was scarcely less important.

As sound recording and reproduction improved, live orchestras were no longer needed in the cinemas but could be recorded. For decades the main movie houses producing films had their own house orchestras and composers who wrote for the movies. Even today, though your attention may mostly be focussed on what you are watching on the big screen, when you go to a film the music plays a major role in the emotions you feel during the film. *Jaws* is just not so scary without those low notes on the cellos and basses, and sentimental 'weepy' films are unlikely to make you shed tears without the accompanying soundtrack of the poignant melody.

Look out for DVD extras on more recent films which sometimes include a feature on the music written for the film. Steven Spielberg's film *Catch me if you can* (2002) with music by John Williams, is one such release with some very interesting footage about the way the music was created to enhance the mood of the film.

 ## Listening ideas

Of the hundreds of composers who have written for the tens of thousands of films that this section of the GCSE specification potentially covers, look out for the following composers' work. These are some of the major composers who have worked in film over the last half-century or more. For each one, a selection of some of their best-known film scores is given.

- Max Steiner (1888–1971): *King Kong* (1933)
  Gone with the Wind (1939)
- Erich Korngold (1897–1957): *The Adventures of Robin Hood* (1938)
  The Sea Hawk (1940)
- Ennio Morricone (b. 1928): *The Good, the Bad and the Ugly* (1966)
  The Mission (1986)
  The Untouchables (1987)

■	Jerry Goldsmith (1929–2004):	*Planet of the Apes* (1968)
		The Russia House (1990)
		Star Trek: Voyager (1995)
■	John Williams (b. 1932):	*Jaws* (1975)
		Star Wars (1977)
		Raiders of the Lost Ark (1981)
		Schindler's List (1993)
		The Terminal (2004)
■	John Barry (b. 1933):	*Goldfinger* (1964)
		Out of Africa (1985)
		Enigma (2001)
■	Philip Glass (b. 1937):	*The Hours* (2002)
		Notes on a Scandal (2006)
■	Vangelis (b. 1943):	*Chariots of Fire* (1981)
		Blade Runner (1982)
■	Michael Nyman (b. 1944):	*The Piano* (1993)
		The End of the Affair (1999)
■	Gabriel Yared (b. 1949):	*The English Patient* (1996)
		The Talented Mr. Ripley (1999)
		Cold Mountain (2003).

'Hedwig's Theme' from *Harry Potter and the Philosopher's Stone* (1997) – John Williams

Hedwig's Theme is available on Music from the Harry Potter Films Silva Screen SILCD1206

The mysterious and magical world of Harry Potter is immediately captured by the bell-like, children's 'Music Box' timbre with which this piece opens. Listen more carefully, though, to the moments that chords change: they are all minor chords, though not necessarily 'belonging' in the traditional sense to the home key of E minor. For instance, in the second phrase the music moves from the chord of E minor to one of G minor and then one of F minor. Both these chords require flats that do not appear in the key of E minor.

All these minor chords create a rather cold and curious atmosphere. This is further enhanced when the tune is then heard on the french horns while the violins are quietly scurrying up and down scales; it is as though they are sliding on ice.

The main theme itself is worth considering for a moment. It has the habit of leaping up or down rather unpredictably, as though we don't know when the next twist or turn is coming. This helps to add to the magical flavour of the music.

A secondary theme is initially heard on woodwinds – oboes and clarinet – and then taken up by the brass. It starts with a repeating note in quavers, and then moves away from this note by a semitone either side, an effect that adds to the creepiness of the sound here.

It is important to have an ear for the different layers in the texture when listening to film music. Note that while the brass take up this secondary theme in mid register, the low strings contribute some scurrying around at the bottom of the texture.

WORLD MUSIC

If Western Classical Music is a broad area of music-making due to the historical dimension of 1,000 years of music-making, World Music is equally broad, but this time due to the geographical dimension: the world really is full of music, each continent, each country, even each village or tribe having its own musical tradition. Of the many traditions of World Music, AQA have selected three for you to explore:

- Music of the Caribbean
- Music of Africa
- Music of India.

Once again, there are no set works or compulsory albums that you must know. Instead there is an opportunity to go on a journey – if not actually to these three areas of the world – nonetheless a journey of exploration to discover these areas through their musical traditions.

This should enable you to be able to tell the difference aurally between music of the three regions and to explain this difference through the way the music uses each of the elements of music.

 Resources

Recommended resources for this Strand include:

Books:

- *The Rough Guide to World Music: vol. 1 – Africa, Europe and the Middle East*
- *The Rough Guide to World Music: vol. 2 – Latin and North America, Caribbean, India, Asia and Pacific*

Recordings:

- *Music of the Caribbean* – Various Artists (Mra) 2005
- *World of Music: Caribbean* – Various Artists (Hallmark) 2003
- *The Rough Guide to Central America* – Various Artists
- *The Very Best of Africa vol. 1* – Various Artists (Nascente) 2006
- *The Very Best of Africa vol. 2* – Various Artists (Nascente) 2004
- *The Very Best of India* – Various Artists (Nascente) 2003.

MUSIC OF THE CARIBBEAN

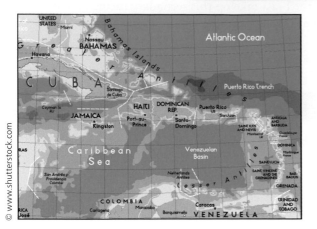

The Caribbean is a sea between the coast of Central America and a line of islands, some large such as Cuba and others much smaller such as Barbados, which separates the Caribbean from the Atlantic Ocean.

The region is named after one of the tribes that inhabited many of the smaller islands that are collectively known as the Lesser Antilles. Once the region was discovered by Europeans, new influences arrived, not just with European settlers, but also with the African people who the Europeans took there to be slaves. The last people to speak the original Carib language died out in the 1920s.

Traditional Garifuna percussion instruments include:

A tenor drum: the **Primero**

A bass drum: the **Segunda**

Various shakers made from seed-filled gourds, called **Sisera**

The drum skins traditionally come from the skin of the peccary, a wild pig.

Nowadays there are a variety of musical traditions in the region; in many cases each island has its own specific tradition. The examples below should give you a broad experience of styles from the Caribbean region and enable you to identify an excerpt met in the exam as Caribbean rather than African or Indian, as well as helping you to identify typical features.

'Dance of the Junka Stick' (from *World of Music: Caribbean* – Hallmark, ASIN: B0000A1M7I)

This is a good introduction to many of the features of Caribbean music. The whole song is built on a simple chord sequence of I–IV–I–V which is used without harmonic change 40 times over, each chord lasting for one bar.

As the song is in a major key (E♭), by only using these three chords (I, IV and V) the harmony of the song is consistently major in colour. The positive, cheerful flavour this creates is reinforced by the riff pattern in the bass which uses rising broken chord patterns in bars 1–3, before a falling scale in bar 4 leading back to the tonic.

This very repetitive basis for the song is given variety and Caribbean colour through the use of various timbres. Some of these on the recording are generated electronically. The main elements of the instrumentation that you should listen out for are:

- A soft, sustained 'synth pad' (played on the synthesiser or keyboard)
- Steel pans: the 'signature' instrument of Caribbean music
- Guitar: which plays crisp, short chords on beats 2 and 4, a feature associated with reggae
- Trumpets: playing short melodic ideas based around the chords
- Drums and other percussion
- Voice (singer).

The following chart shows the way that these timbres are treated to a 'mix and match' approach:

Phrase	Synth	Pans	Guitar	Trumpets	Drums	Singer
1–2	✓	✓				
3–4	✓	✓				
5–6	✓	✓	✓		✓	
7–8	✓	✓	✓		✓	
9–10			✓		✓	✓
11–12			✓		✓	✓
13–14	✓	✓	✓		✓	
15–16	✓	✓	✓		✓	
17–18		✓	✓	✓	✓	
19–20		✓	✓	✓	✓	
21–22		✓	✓		✓	✓
23–24		✓	✓		✓	✓
25–26			✓	✓	✓	
27–28		✓	✓	✓	✓	
29–30	✓	✓				
31–32	✓	✓	✓			
33–34		✓	✓	✓	✓	
35–36		✓	✓	✓	✓	
37–38	✓	✓	✓	✓	✓	
39–40	✓	✓	✓	✓	✓	

Many of these features are found in arguably the most typical of all Caribbean styles, Calypso. A good example is 'Fire' by the band New Revelation from the Central American country of Costa Rica which is included on the *Rough Guide to the Music of Central America*.

Listen out for the following details:

- The repetitive chord pattern of primary triads: I–IV–V–I
- **Syncopation** in the melodic lines
- The accompaniment on strummed guitar and bongos.

'Alaporio' by Titiman Flores (from *Rough Guide to the Music of Central America* RGNET1077)

Titiman Flores comes from Belize, one of the countries of Central America with a coastline on the Caribbean Sea. Along with neighbouring countries such as Guatemala, Honduras and Nicaragua, Belize is home to the **Garifuna** people, who are of mixed ancestry, blending Carib and African blood.

Early in Garifuna history their musical style, known as paranda, was based on unpitched percussion instruments. Some traditional paranda music has been recorded since the 1990s. By then other instruments, especially the guitar, which came with Spanish colonial rule, had combined for a new style known as **punta**. Subsequent addition of synthesisers and other electric instruments took this a stage further to a style known as **punta rock** which is represented by this song.

Titiman Flores is one of the leading exponents of the style; his music is deeply rooted in Garifuna culture. His band, the Punta Rockers, includes his daughter on bass guitar.

Alaporio, sung in the Garifuna language, captures the energy for which Flores is well known, despite a minor key being used for the song. The energy is largely due to the brisk tempo and constant percussion backing.

The song alternates instrumental and sung sections. The instrumental sections feature a bold melody played on a trumpet-like synthesized timbre in which a rising triad and repeated notes are prominent.

The sung passages make great use of call and response textures in which the solo singer (Flores) is answered by a small group of male voices in unison. This verse section is in two halves: in the first half the call and answer are of equal length; in the second half the 'chorus' just repeat the final few notes of each solo phrase.

The harmonic content of the song relies on just two chords: the tonic (F♯ minor) and the dominant 7th (C♯⁷). At the end there is a lengthy passage of just the tonic chord as the song fades out.

'Bruca Maniguá' (from *Ibrahim Ferrer* – WCD055)

This song is of a style known as **son** which was developed in the Caribbean's largest island, and one of its most musical: Cuba.

Son was popular between the 1920s and the 1950s, gaining a worldwide popularity, and blended a type of Spanish song (cancíon) and the Spanish love of the guitar with African rhythms and percussion instruments that had become popular in the Caribbean due to the slave trade.

Due to the politics of Cuba in the second half of the 20th century which provoked a very long American embargo, modern influences have had little impact in Cuba. Thus when American guitarist Ry Cooder made it to Cuba in 1996 he was able to record the famous album *Buena Vista Social Club*: a collection of the old son hits performed in the old-fashioned way by, largely, aging musicians who had been playing them all their lives. Among them was the singer Ibrahim Ferrer, who was already 69 years old.

Such was the success of the *Buena Vista Social Club* album that Ry Cooder returned to Cuba to make another album starring Ferrer in 1999 on which 'Bruca Maniguá' is the first track. Ferrer's last album made shortly before his death in 2005 and released the following year.

The song opens with a lengthy instrumental introduction that features an expressive, lyrical violin melody in four-bar phrases in a slow duple metre. This opens with some rising upbeats and then a long C (over a bar long) which is heard over the tonic chord of E♭ major. This creates a sense of longing, since we sense that sooner or later it must fall to the more consonant B♭ (the 5th of the chord).

The harmony is slow to move; the entire opening four-bar phrase is over chord I, and the second phrase starts with two bars of chord I before moving to chord V.

As soon as the first downbeat is reached, listen out for the pervasive rhythmic pattern in the accompaniment:

This rhythm pattern is very similar to the Afro-Caribbean Habanera dance rhythm.

Note also how the piano often fills the slightly static moment between the first and second notes of this pattern with a discreet figure. The violin has the third phrase, though this is answered by trumpets, still in a dreamy mood.

The second half of the introduction has a different harmonic colour as significant use is made of the minor chord VI (C minor) as well as chord V. The violin again takes the melody; the two trumpets are now used to provide small interjections (starting on the offbeat) in 3rds.

The rhythmic figure continues through the verse when the singer enters. The melody has a similar phrase structure and harmonic shape to the introduction, but the violin is silent and only in the second half do the trumpets play a little with their syncopated figure in 3rds.

A doubling of the tempo at 2'28" marks the start of the more upbeat second half in which more percussion is heard: especially scrapers and shakers. At 3'06" a solo trumpet comes to the fore, and this is answered by the solo violin from 3'28". Listen out for the section between 3'42" and 3'50" in which the violin's melody involves every interval between a 2nd and the octave with one exception: can you hear which one is missing?

'En tus manos' – Milly Quezada (available on *20 Exitos originales,* and on YouTube)

Milly Quezada was born in Santo Domingo, capital of the Dominican Republic and is considered to be the 'Queen of Merengue'. **Merengue** is a fast, highly rhythmic dance style from the Dominican Republic and its neighbouring country of French-speaking Haiti (together the two comprise the island of Hispaniola, the second largest island in the Caribbean). The merengue is usually in $\frac{2}{4}$ time and has a strong rhythm section, typically comprising:

- Congas – a pair of tall drums, perhaps derived from barrels, played by hand
- Güira – a sheet of metal with bumps made into a cylinder than is scraped, especially on the downbeat.

In addition, there is a major role for a brass section, typically with some high trumpets interjecting, and a piano. Modern merengue practice also includes saxophone, backing singers and bass guitar.

'En tus manos' (In Your Hands) exhibits all these aspects. Listen out, in particular, for the energetic and syncopated brass passages around 1'30" and 2'20".

Congas

Common percussion instruments in Cuban music include:

Bongos: two small drums, untuned but of different pitch, played by hand

Claves: two sticks usually of rosewood or ebony that give a distinct 'clicking' sound

Maracas: the most common form of shaker, traditionally a dried gourd or coconut shell with dried beans or seeds inside.

'Is This Love?' – Bob Marley (available on *Legend: the Best of Bob Marley*)

Bob Marley is probably the most famous musician to have come from the Caribbean; his album, *EXODUS,* was chosen by *TIME* magazine as the greatest of the 20th century. The compilation album *Legend* is the best-selling reggae album of all time.

© Getty Images

Bob Marley

Born in Jamaica in 1945, Marley is, above all, associated with the Jamaican style reggae, to which 'Is This Love?' is a good introduction. It first appeared in 1978 on Marley's album, *Kaya*. Among the features to listen out for are:

- The slow, steady tempo: reggae takes a slower beat than the early Jamaican style of ska, from which it was derived
- The stressing of strong beats (beats 1 and 3) in the percussion
- Staccato chords on beats 2 and 4 (the backbeats) played on a particular early kind of electronic organ known as a Hammond organ
- High-pitched untuned percussion timbres
- The use of backing singers
- Melodic shapes in the bass of the texture.

Also listen out for the triplet rhythms in the vocal line at the lyric 'Is This love?' which brings out an entrancing laid-back character in the music typical of the reggae style.

MUSIC OF AFRICA

Having already found a wide variety of musical styles in the Caribbean, we now turn to the next area of World Music set by AQA: a whole continent – Africa.

Clearly this is a huge area of the world: the planet's second-largest continent comprising 61 states and nearly 15% of the world's population. Of course, over this huge area there is a wide range of musical styles to be explored. The examples given below inevitably only dip a toe in the water, but have been chosen to give as wide a range as possible. Their countries of origin are shown on this map:

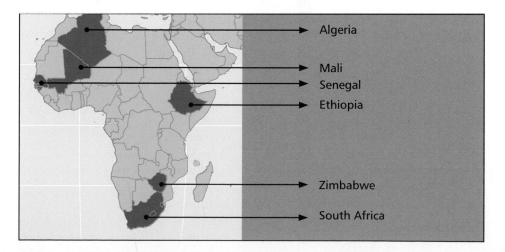

'Didi' – Khaled (Algeria) (available on *The Very Best of Africa* vol. 1 disc 1, ASIN: B00005QD0X)

Khaled himself has said 'In raï music people can express themselves. We break taboos.'

Khaled (b. 1960) is one of the most successful Algerian musicians working in the style known as **raï**, a folk style that originated in the city of Oran on the Mediterranean coast in the 1930s. More recently, it has become the voice of the progressive movements in Algeria, dealing with modern social issues and influenced by western electronic instruments, and a source of provocation to the fundamentalist Islamic elements in the country.

Raï music has become very popular in France – the former colonial power of Algeria – where there is a sizeable Algerian community. 'Didi' was the first Arabic song to reach number one in the French charts (in 1992).

A timeline of the song's structure is as follows:

Khaled

- 0'00"   The song starts with a passage of rhythmic music for untuned percussion that is typically African
- 0'05"   While the percussion music continues, a melodic line starts that immediately suggest the Arab world due to the rather coarse reedy timbre of the *zurna* (a wind instrument somewhat like the medieval shawm), the modal melodic shape that has the compass of an augmented 4th – a rather exotic and brash interval, and the spirited rhythmic character
  (The outline of the melody is as follows:)

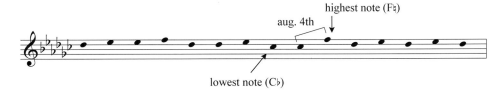

- 0'15"   Khaled enters with an introductory vocal section, almost to a single note in chanted style
- 0'32"   A sampled drum track and bass part enters
- 0'42"   Verse 1 starts
- 0'59"   An instrumental chorus with reedy wind instrument
- 1'14"   Verse 2 starts
- 1'30"   Instrumental chorus
- 1'45"   Verse 3
- 2'06"   Saxophone solo
- 2'31"   Verse 4
- 2'49"   Instrumental chorus
- 3'03"   Verse 5
- 3'20"   Instrumental chorus
- 3'35"   Verse 6
- 3'52"   Instrumental chorus
- 4'06"   Verse 7
- 4'23"   Instrumental chorus plus saxophone solo, fading to the end.

Listen out carefully for the formula that ends each verse and announces the forthcoming chorus: most of each verse is to a static bass note and chord, but each time the bass and/or the chords move two steps down and then back again, and does this pattern twice before going into the chorus.

This is a very successful fusion of traditional African and Arabic elements (the opening drumming, the melodic contours, the zurna in the chorus) with western influences (the sampled drum track, bass guitar and saxophone solo).

'Salama' – Toumani Diabaté and Ballake Sissoko (Mali) (Available on *The Very Best of Africa* vol. 1 disc 2)

© Getty Images

Toumani Diabaté

Mali is one of Africa's most musical countries. Among its treasures is the kora: an instrument that is something of a cross between a lute and a harp. The kora is made from a large calabash (a type of vegetable gourd that can be dried and used as a water carrier, or, in this instance, resonator for a musical instrument when cut in half and covered in a cow's hide). Over this are arranged 21 strings: 11 for the left hand and 10 for the right. These are plucked by the thumb and first finger of each hand. The resulting sound is very beautiful and sweet; music for kora tends to involve some riffs and also solo passages that sounds like cascades of notes. Skilled players can play both these roles simultaneously.

Kora players in Mali traditionally belonged to certain families, known as griots, and learned their music from their forefathers. Toumani Diabaté is Mali's top virtuoso kora player and his father, Sidiki, was known as 'the King of the kora'. He was born in the Malian capital, Bamako, in 1965. 'Salama' appeared on his fifth album, *New Ancient Strings*, on which he collaborated with a distant cousin, Ballake Sissoko.

'Salama' is an instrumental composition inspired by a poignant love song called 'Tita'. There is a short, slow introduction that has something of an improvised character with no clear pulse. Then at 0'23" a repeating ostinato pattern in the bass appears (D–C–D–C–E–C–E–C in which the Ds and Es are long notes) which repeats without variation for the remainder of the six-minute track. Over the top are spun intricate melodies on the kora that bring out a mellow, minor flavour and an elegant, tender mood. The full range of the instrument is thoroughly explored: listen for some lower register phrases after the 2' mark, and again from 4'10". Whilst the ostinato pattern (or riff) maintains a regular rhythm, the melodic material spins very freely in all manner of complex rhythms. The combination is very hypnotic and beautiful.

'Kowoni Maayo' – Baaba Maal (Senegal) (Available on *The Very Best of Africa* vol. 2 disc 2, ASIN: B00002FUI38)

Many of Mali's musical traditions are shared with neighbouring Senegal on the west coast of Africa. Several of the features heard in the previous kora piece from Mali can be heard in this song by the Senegalese singer and guitarist Baaba Maal (b. 1953). The song was recorded on his most chilled album to date, *Missing You*, released in 2001. Particular features in common with 'Salama' are:

- There is a slow-moving, improvisatory introduction
- At 30" a regularly repeating bass pattern commences (in this case slow notes alternating between A and B) which continues uninterrupted for the remainder of the song
- Over the top various intricate guitar melodies are spun, as well as (in this case) the vocal line.

In addition, there is plenty of interest in the use of percussion here, largely on hand-played drums, which gives away the music's African origin. Listen out, in particular, for the patterns at 4'25". Use is also made of a distant and wordless female voice, initially in the introduction and then again at around 2'10".

'Ethiopia' – Gigi and Abyssinia Infinite (Ethiopia) (Available on *The Very Best of Africa* vol. 2 disc 2)

This song from the war-torn and famine-stricken country of Ethiopia shares some of the features of the Senegalese song, in particular the repeating riff pattern (in this case G–A–G–B–G–A–G), but the strings sound of the kora or guitar is not present. Instead keyboards are used, with the riff played on a warm clarinet tone, and a soft string pad used for a sustained effect in the background.

Although the riff is repetitive and the sustained harmony has little change, there is a beauty in this music through the subtle rhythmic interplay of the various elements, especially the intricate vocal line which uses a lot of melisma and has quite a mesmerizing affect.

The harmony of the song is consistently G major, but various notes sound against this, including the A in the riff pattern and some notes that emerge in the sustained backdrop or the vocal line.

'Chemutengure' – Thomas Mapfumo (Zimbabwe) (Available on *The Very Best of Africa* vol. 2 disc 2)

Thomas Mapfumo was born in 1945 and developed a style of music he called 'chimurenga', a word from the Zimbabwean language of Shona meaning 'struggle'. (He often sings in the Shona language too.) This reflected the fact that he used his music in the crusade for Zimbabwean independence from its British colonial

Mbira

past and the 'white' government that assumed power upon independence. Sadly, Mapfumo subsequently fled into exile from the Mugabe regime and now lives in America.

One of Mapfumo's skills is playing the Mbira, a traditional instrument in Zimbabwe in which metal prongs are fixed to a board and then flicked by the player's thumbs, each one producing a different note. This can be heard at the start of *Chemtengure*. A guitar and drums soon join in, but the mbira keeps up a regular percussive plucking effect throughout the song.

Thomas Mapfumo

Mapfumo starts singing at 0'21"; the melodic lines comprises a short falling phrase which is repeated many times trough the song. After each solo verse a chorus involving a handful of other voices takes over. The singing is broken up by a brief guitar solo at 2'42".

Throughout there is a repetitive chord pattern of IV–I–V–I (in D major). The combination of this progression of major triads and the regular clicking of the mbira creates a very upbeat flavour to the song.

'Homeless' – Ladysmith Black Mambazo (South Africa) (Available on *The Very Best of Africa* vol. 1 disc 2)

Ladysmith Black Mambazo is a male choral group from South Africa of worldwide renown. They perform in an *a cappella* style (without accompaniment) known as **mbube**. The effect is very striking and moving; they captured something of a resilient spirit during the struggle against the apartheid regime up to 1991.

'Homeless' was a song on the 1986 album *Graceland* by American singer-songwriter Paul Simon that involved Ladysmith Black Mambazo. There is a typically South African (in particular, Zulu) flavour to the singing here with solo lines answered by homophonic choral responses, and a choral texture dominated by warm, rich bass voices, coupled with lighter higher register voices.

MUSIC OF INDIA

This third and last area of World Music set by AQA is a single country rather than a region or whole continent. India is, however, the seventh largest country in the world and the second most populous nation on the planet. It is, therefore, rich and diverse in its musical traditions.

As in the west, India has a tradition of classical music as well as more popular styles. The classical tradition is quite different to western classical music in virtually all ways: the instruments used, the tuning of notes, and the methods of constructing a piece. There are two main traditions of Indian classical music: Hindustani music from the north of the country, and Carnatic music from the south.

The concepts behind Indian Classical Music can seem very foreign to people whose musical experience is wholly western. The music is essentially monophonic: a single melodic line that is usually played over a fixed drone with some rhythmic element provided on the tabla (a pair of hand-played drums of different pitch). Each piece will be based on a series of notes known as a **raga**.

There are a huge number of available ragas and many have special significance such as being connected to a certain time of day or season of the year. The raga is the basis from which musicians create melodic lines during a piece. Both Hindustani and Carnatic music use ragas, though often they have their own ragas for each context, with only some shared in common. The most significant note in a raga is known as the *Vadi* (King note) and the second most significant note as the *Samavadi* (Queen note). These notes with receive a more emphasised treatment when they occur.

The rhythm in Indian classical music is also organised in a different way to Western music. In place of metre and time signature, is a system known as **tala**, which creates a rhythmic cycle. Two of the most common are *tintal*, which is a pattern of four groups of four beats in which the first, second and fourth groups are accented while the third is light; and *ektal* which takes more than a minute for its 12 beats.

Instruments used in Indian classical music include:

- Hindustani tradition:
  - Sitar – a long-necked lute with sympathetic strings and distinctive resonance
  - Sarod – another Indian lute with sympathetic strings, but no frets
  - Tanpura – a long-necked lute that is used to provide the drone
  - Bansuri – a bamboo flute
  - Shehnai – a wind instrument from Kashmir using two double reeds
  - Sarangi – a short-necked lute that is played with a bow, resembling the sound of the human voice
  - Tabla – a pair of drums played by hand, with contrasting pitch.

- Carnatic tradition:
  - Venu – a bamboo flute from south India
  - Gottuvadyam – a complex instrument with 21 strings, including three drones and six for melodies
  - Veena – a plucked lute
  - Mridangam – a double-headed drum
  - Kanjira – an Indian type of tambourine used in Carnatic music since the 1930s
  - Ghatam – a percussion instrument in the form of an earthenware pot.

Sitar

Indian popular music covers a wide range of folk styles, the best-known of which is Bhangra from the Punjab region and commonly associated with those of the Sikh faith. This style is dominated by an elaborate rhythmic played on the dhol, a double-headed drum, and also involves singing and playing of plucked single string instruments called the iktar and the tumbi.

In more recent times, the spread of pop music from the west has brought new influences to Indian popular music, and some artists have tried to fuse elements of traditional Indian styles with technology-based western sounds. The huge success of the Bollywood film industry based in Mumbai has been another area of considerable musical activity.

Those wanting a flavour of Bollywood-style music should watch the Oscar-winning film *Slumdog Millionaire*, and in particular the closing credits.

'Raga Devgiri Bilawal' – Ravi Shankar (available on *The Very Best of India* disc 2, ASIN: B0000A59MG)

Ravi Shankar

Ravi Shankar is the most famous Indian musician and player of the sitar of the 20th century. He was born in 1920 and founded a society for Hindustani musicians called the Maihar gharana. In his long career he worked with a wide range of leading musicians from other musical cultures including the western classical violinist Yehudi Menuhin, the Beatles musician George Harrison and traditional Japanese flute player Hozan Yamamoto. His most important collaboration, however, has been with the tabla player Alla Rakha who plays on this track.

'Raga Devgiri Bilawal' opens with just the sound of the sitar. Listen carefully to the music to hear the drone that is present quite softly in the background. Over this there are various improvised melodic shapes, some that include some pitch-bending achieved by manipulating the strings. There is little sense of a pulse, instead considerable rhythmic freedom, and the effect is quite dreamy. This is a traditional way of starting a piece in Hindustani music and the name for such a slow, improvised opening is the **alap**.

A flourish at 1'38" marks the entry of the tabla. The rhythms that they bring to the music create a much more regular sense of beat and a faster tempo. There are some remarkable intricate drumming rhythms and from this moment on the sitar melodies are much more animated. Try to listen to the piece twice concentrating on each instrument in turn. The music really sparkles and the effect is quite hypnotic. By the end the playing of both musicians is quite frenzied.

© Getty Images

'Guru Bandana' – Ali Akbar Khan and Asha Bhosle (available on *The Very Best of India* disc 2)

Asha Bhosle

Ali Akbar Khan is a Bengali musician born in 1922 who is a master Sarod player. In this track he collaborates with Asha Bhosle who is renowned as a singer for the sound tracks in Bollywood movies.

'Guru Bandana' is intended to be a musical prayer that expresses the devotional relationship between a guru and a pupil. The atmosphere is slow and reverential throughout. There is a lengthy introduction for the sarod alone, giving you a chance to hear the different tone quality that the sarod has from the better known (in the west) sitar. Listen out particularly for the rich tenor register notes from 0'30" onwards. At times these almost imitate the human voice.

The singer enters at 2'05" and maintains the spiritual character of the music. Listen carefully for the different ways Asha Bhosle uses her voice, including:

- Some lyrics, some wordless singing
- Sustained low notes
- Melisma, often involving rapid, ornamented changes of note
- Changes of dynamic
- Pitch bending
- Humming.

There is a short interlude in the singing at 4'00" during which the sarod comes to the fore with melodic material again. The singer then re-enters to finish the piece.

'Signs' – Badmarsh and Shri (available on *The Very Best of India* disc 1)

Badmarsh and Shri are a duo of Indian origin working in London. They comprise a bansuri flute player, Shrikanth 'Shri' Sriram and tabla player Aref 'Badmarsh' Durvesh. 'Signs' is the title track from their second album released in 2001.

The timeline of the song is as follows:

- 0'00"   Electronic sound effects start
- 0'02"   Sampled alternating two-note pattern on the bansuri flute is heard
- 0'10"   Six-note string pattern that is used as a riff before the rest of the introduction starts. This comprises two sets of three descending notes: G–F♯–E and G–F♯–D.
  Also, a sampled vibraphone pattern is used
- 0'20"   Digital drum track starts. There is also some distant sampled vocal material

Tabla

■	0'53"	Intro ends; Verse I is sung. This is accompanied by the tabla and bass
■	1'14"	Interlude using material from the intro, especially the six-note string riff
■	1'36"	Verse 2 is sung, now to the accompaniment of the digital drum track instead of the tabla, and involving bass guitar too
■	2'19"	A long interlude that is re-mixed from previous sections. The bass is heard from the start of the section; listen out too for the distant sampled vocals at 2'29", the tabla from 3'00" and the vibraphone from 3'03"
■	3'34"	Verse 3
■	4'17"	The singing stops and a collage of sampled tracks ends the song.

UNIT 1: LISTENING TO AND APPRAISING MUSIC

WHAT DOES IT INVOLVE?

This is the only unit of your GCSE music that is like a traditional exam and is worth 20% of the total GCSE marks. All pupils across the country taking the AQA GCSE music exam will sit this unit at the same time, and so you will be with your fellow students in an exam room at your school or centre.

However, there is one big difference between this unit and any other GCSE examinations that you may be taking in other subjects: in this unit you will hear music in the exam room. This obviously means that the room in which you take this exam can only be used for the music GCSE exam at the official time this unit must be sat; therefore you may well find that you have to go to a different room (maybe in your music department) for this exam: make sure you are well organised for this.

There will be a series of excerpts of music that will be played to you on a CD. These pieces of music will be chosen to highlight the Areas of Study.

Each of these will be played more than once with short silences in between; typically you will hear each extract 2–4 times. On the question paper there will be a set of questions about each piece of music you hear. These questions will:

- Require careful listening to the music
- Include some musical notation of the music to which you listen
- Be answered on the question paper
- Involve some multiple-choice questions
- Involve some short answer questions
- Involve some extended answer questions
- Involve writing some missing notes onto the notation provided.

IN THE EXAM ROOM

One implication of how this exam works is that you need to be ready to answer each question at the rate at which the relevant music is played on the CD. It will not be possible to go back to an earlier question and hear the music again. It is therefore very important to use the period of two minutes before the CD is started to read through the paper and prepare for the task ahead. One useful practical thing might be to highlight the Areas of Study on which each question focuses. This should help you to get your thoughts quickly geared towards the kind of issues that go with those particular Areas of Study before you even hear the music for the first time.

Top Tips

You will be expected to answer most questions in **black** ink or **black** ballpoint pen. However, you are allowed to use pencil when you have to write musical notation. This often helps your answer look legible, especially if you change your mind from your first attempted answer (so long as you have a rubber with you).

At the end of the CD there will be a period of silence during which you can read through your answers and look for obvious mistakes; however, be cautious about changing your answers now, since you will not be able to hear the music again at this point. It may well be that your initial instinct when you were listening to the music being played is more reliable than a last-minute recollection of what you think you remember hearing.

On the other hand, if you left any answers completely blank, you might as well try an answer of some sort at this point: maybe you'll spot a clue you missed in the given score that helps you, or the right technical term may suddenly come to you when earlier on your mind went blank. Failing all else you might as well make a guess: it might be that your luck's in and you earn a valuable extra mark, which you certainly won't get if you leave an answer blank for the examiner.

However, don't write more than you are asked for. If the question asks you to identify one instrument and you write two or three answers because you're not sure, you won't get any marks even if one of them is correct.

PREPARING FOR THE EXAM

General preparation

You can't start preparing for this paper too early: it is more an examination of a skill (listening) than of knowledge. Training your ear to listen acutely and perceptively cannot be done overnight. Like an athlete tuning the muscles relevant to their particular sport, you need to use your ears regularly in this way

© www.shutterstock.com

over a sustained period: ideally the two years most people will take to cover the GCSE course.

There is some useful general advice about listening in the Introduction section of this guide (page 7). Clearly, it is best to factor into your weekly routine some properly focused and varied listening to music via recordings, radio, downloads, or live concerts. However, there are many times we hear music in modern life and these can offer unexpected opportunities for training your aural perception.

Listening ideas

For instance, if you hear a mobile phone ring-tone going off on the bus, you could tune into the sound and consider the following questions (among others):

- Does the ring-tone have an ascending or descending melodic contour?
- Is it all at the same dynamic (volume)?
- Can you clap the pulse of the ring tone?
- Can you clap the actual rhythm of the tone?
- Do you only hear a single melody line, or is there more than a single note at any one time?

It is interesting that phones are sometimes described as having the potential to play 'polyphonic' ring tones. You might like to consider to what extent this is an accurate musical use of the term (see page 52).

Other opportunities that you might come across are: emergency vehicle alarms (what is the interval between the notes involved?), attention-grabbing tones before PA announcements, your school bell (how would you know it from other school bells?), jingles that play when computer programs are opened or used, music in lifts and so on.

As your exam draws near, you will want to do some more specific revision geared to the subject content of the AQA GCSE specification. You may be wondering about the best way to do this: should you concentrate on the Areas of Study, or on the Strands?

It is crucial that you make sure that you are listening to music that represents all three Strands, and within each one all the relevant subsections. More significant, however, is the fact that each question is designed to target specific Areas of Study. As the exam approaches this provides the most methodical way of preparing yourself.

Here is a table of specialist terms for each Area of Study to test yourself on your understanding:

AoS1	AoS2	AoS3	AoS4	AoS5
Rhythm and metre	**Harmony and Tonality**	**Texture and Melody**	**Timbre and Dynamics**	**Structure and Form**
Pulse	Diatonic	Homophonic	Pizzicato	Binary
Simple time	Chromatic	Polyphonic	Arco	Ternary
Compound time	Consonant	Contrapuntal	Con sordini	Rondo
Irregular/Free time	Dissonant	Imitation	Double-stopping	Theme and
Augmentation	Pedal & drone	Canon	Tremolo/	Variations
Diminution	Cadences	Unison	tremolando	Sonata form
Triplets	Tierce de Picardie	Octaves	Falsetto	Minuet and Trio
Hemiola	Tonal	Single melody line	Vibrato	Ground bass
Cross-rhythm	Major	Antiphonal	Countertenor	Concerto
Rubato	Minor	Intervals	Reverb	Cadenza
Polyrhythm	Modal	Conjunct	Distortion	Call & Response
Drum fills	Key signatures	Disjunct	Chorus	32-bar song form
	Modulation	Triadic	Crescendo	Pop ballad
		Scalic	Diminuendo	
		Arpeggio	Sforzando	
		Passing note		
		Acciaccatura		
		Appoggiatura		
		Blue notes		
		Pentatonic		
		Whole tone		
		Sequence		
		Inversion		
		Glissando		
		Portamento		
		Ostinato		
		Riff		
		Pitch bend		

Use the Areas of Study section of this book (pages 9–62) to check any of these terms for which you are unsure.

Typical questions for each Area of Study include:

Area of Study 1 – Rhythm and Metre

■ Suggest an appropriate tempo marking
■ Identify the time signature

- Spot what rhythmic pattern is being used*
- Completing the notation of rhythm where some notes are omitted
- Identify rhythmic devices (e.g. syncopation, polyrhythm, drum fill, etc).*

Area of Study 2 – Harmony and Tonality

- Identify the kind of tonality (major, minor, modal, pentatonic, etc)
- Spot when a modulation has occurred
- Identify which kind of cadence is used
- Say which harmonic device has been used (Tierce de picardie, drone, dissonance, etc).*

Area of Study 3 – Texture and Melody

- Identify intervals in a melody
- Identify melodic devices (scales, arpeggios, blue notes, sequence, etc)*
- Complete the notation of a melody where a few notes have been omitted
- Analyse the structure of a melody by its constituent phrases (AABB, ABAB, ABAC, etc).*

Area of Study 4 – Timbre and Dynamics

- Identify which instrument(s) is playing
- Identify types of ensemble or groups of instrument
- Identify use of instrumental techniques*
- Suggest suitable dynamics to match a performance.

Area of Study 5 – Structure and Form

- Indicate where new sections start (possibly on a chart)
- Identify a structural device (ground bass, cadenza, etc).*

*Indicates a question that is likely to be presented as a multiple-choice question.

UNIT 2: COMPOSING AND APPRAISING MUSIC

WHAT DOES IT INVOLVE?

This unit brings together many aspects of the GCSE course and is worth 20% of the total GCSE marks. There are two, equally weighted parts to the unit.

Firstly, you have to compose an original piece of music that meets the following requirements:

- It should be stimulated by two or more of the Areas of Study
- There should be a link to the Strand stipulated by AQA each year
- The piece should demonstrate that you have developed your initial musical ideas
- There should be a score of your composition

■ There should be a recording of your composition.

Secondly, you must complete a written appraisal of your composition, covering both the way you went about writing the piece, and the success of the finished composition. This takes the form of a printed booklet supplied by AQA that you have to complete.

COMPLETING THE UNIT

There are some very particular regulations for completing this unit, which your school or college will be required to follow.

The **composition** has to be completed in 20 hours of **controlled time**. This can be scheduled at your school's discretion. If you have friends at another school you may find that they have started their controlled time before you: there is no particular 'best' way; it is more a case of what suits your school's routine. You may have 20 one-hour sessions, or 10 two-hour sessions, and so forth. In this time you will be supervised, a little like in an exam room, though you will have the freedom to move between a keyboard or other instruments, a desk and a computer, as you wish. Between sessions your work will be collected and stored by your teacher, since you are not allowed to be working on it outside the official controlled time.

You will be allowed to work on ideas for your piece outside the classroom. For example, you might wish to do some internet research about the type of music you are writing. Or, perhaps, begin to work on an idea by working it out on an instrument. However, you cannot take additional written material into the controlled area.

 Top Tips

Although you cannot take your work home with you between the periods of controlled time, there is nothing to stop you from experimenting with your ideas at home: you will just have to remember what you have achieved and re-create it back in the 'controlled time' room, as you will not be allowed to bring work in with you.

Once the 20 hours of controlled time has finished you are not allowed to alter your composition so by this stage you must have completed the **score**. This can be of various kinds:

■ A fully-notated score in staff notation, showing every note and performance direction that is needed in your piece for a full, musical performance of your composition
■ A score that uses other, well-known representations of music, such as guitar tab
■ A graphic-notation version of your piece, in which the main features of your piece are represented in a diagrammatic form and can be followed logically when listening to the piece

- A written account of your piece that provides a thorough description of structure and content of your piece
- A combination of some or all the above methods.

You should choose whichever method best suits the style of your piece.

The **recording** of your composition can be made during the 20-hour period of controlled time, but can also be done outside this time if you are struggling to finish the composition in the time allowed. The recording must be finalised onto a format that can be sent off to the examiners, such as CD or mini-disc; your teacher can help you with this task.

The **appraisal** must be completed in a further period of controlled time which can last up to 2 hours. You can expect to be asked about the following aspects of your work:

- Which two Areas of Study stimulated your work?
- How can this be seen in your piece?
- How does your composition link to the Strand that AQA stipulated for the year in which you are doing the exam?

PREPARING FOR THE CONTROLLED TIME PERIOD

General preparation

Many people, even highly accomplished musicians with an expertise for performing, find composing to be a very challenging task, and it is crucial that you build up your skills, musical imagination and, above all, confidence before your teacher sets the stopwatch counting down on the period of controlled time. Some ideas for how to do this are given in the Introduction section of this guide (page 7).

Take a moment to think of some of the different types of music you have heard: perhaps an ancient church hymn, a stirring piece of film music, a jazz number that someone at home likes, a chant that is sung at a football ground, the music that is played at your local Indian restaurant, your current favourite song. One could carry on, and on, and on… This is significant, because the ways of putting together the same dozen (or so) notes are infinite, and provide a staggering range of musical styles.

This can be intimidating, for it also suggests that if there are so many different ways of putting notes together, that it must be a complicated skill to put them together in a successful way that is stylistically coherent. In part this is true, but it is also a fantastic opportunity to experiment and use your musical imagination to find new ways of combining notes, and your musical taste to select which of these ways you think are effective.

All this means that composing, like all artistic skills, needs practice, and you should make sure that you are trying to do at least a little composition every week during the period of your GCSE course.

Where to compose

Composing can be done virtually anywhere. There are some particular scenarios that can be helpful:

Resources

- **Using your instrument**: if you have been playing your instrument for some time, you will be able to improvise music through the almost sub-conscious way you can play your instrument. Experiment with what happens if you start playing with your eyes shut: listen carefully to the music you produce and try to capture some of the ideas and repeat them. This can be done in various ways: identically or with some small changes (maybe just the dynamic is different second time, or perhaps the octave), immediately, or after a short passage of something different.
- **Using a computer**: you may well have access to some very helpful composing software at school, or you may want to invest in some at home. The computer is very helpful in allowing you to hear more complicated musical ideas that you cannot easily play. It is often an aid to developing your piece more quickly because of various copy and paste options. Often it is easy to create sequences, or changes of octave or instrumentation through a small adaptation of more basic (and musically repetitive) cut and paste.
- **In silence**: There are times when your instrument or level of playing ability can be a hindrance to good creative thinking. Similarly, the computer only gives an approximation of real instruments and this can limit good musical results. So take time off from your usual way of composing from time to time and try to imagine the music inside your head. This may very well give you inspiration to imagine what happens next.

How to compose

In a moment we shall look at how each Area of Study can be used as a starting point for creating compositional ideas, but first a few general principles.

Composing ideas

There are two different, but equally important ways of thinking that are used in composition:

- **Imaginative thinking**: to devise original musical ideas that are interesting and have musical character
- **Logical thinking**: to see the pattern of the notes in a musical idea, and extend the idea through replicating the pattern and combining it with other patterns.

The best composers combine these two different ways of thinking in their work. Both ways of thinking can be applied to each of the Areas of Study; indeed, it is often very effective to be logical with some Areas of Study while being imaginative with another. For example:

- The **metre** can be consistent and the same rhythmic pattern can be repeated = *logical*
- The **harmony** can alternate major and minor chords = *logical*
- The **texture** can consistently be in two parts = *logical*; but they can swap roles = *imaginative*
- The **melody** can be repeated at a different pitch as a sequence = *logical*, but with an unexpected leap of an octave halfway through the repeated phrase = *imaginative*
- The **timbre** can consistently use the same instrument = *logical*, but an interesting playing technique can be introduced = *imaginative*.

All these descriptions are true of the following four-bar phrase, but could be used on a wider scale:

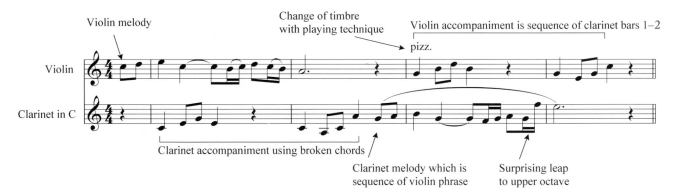

If you only ever use *imaginative* thinking it is likely that every bar will do something unexpected: that there are sudden changes in rhythm, melodic shape, harmony, texture, instrumentation, and so on. The result will be bewildering to the listener and your piece is unlikely to be satisfying.

If you only ever use *logical* thinking it is likely that every bar will be very predictable: that in all aspects – rhythm, melody, harmony, textures, etc. – the same patterns are repeated without variety. The result will be rather boring to the listener and, again, your piece is unlikely to be satisfying.

A good rule of thumb is to think of a relatively short idea, perhaps two bars long, and immediately reuse it so that it registers in the listener's memory. Then try to invent two or four bars that are a little different before returning to your original idea. You have now made a musical sentence.

Your next musical sentence should be a little more different than the middle of the first sentence was to how your piece started, though not radically different. Follow a similar principle to make a second sentence. You may like to add a third sentence or re-use your first sentence. You now have a musical paragraph.

The start of the second musical paragraph is likely to be still more different to the first paragraph. Maybe after this you might like to revisit your first paragraph.

Responding to Rhythm and Metre

Rhythm is very often the most significant element to the way in which music gains a sense of character. Read through the section on Rhythm and Metre in the Introduction, and especially the 'Characteristic rhythm patterns' (on page 16) covering dotted rhythms, triplet rhythms and syncopation.

Often using just one of these strong rhythmic 'flavourings' for a main musical idea is a strong and convincing way forwards, mixing whichever one you choose with some other more straightforward note values. Another similar device is to use rests of short duration (quaver or semiquaver) on the beat; this gives a sense of momentum to the rhythm.

Try to create rhythms that form musical sentences. This tends to require somewhat longer note values at the end of each sentence or phrase.

Clap through the following musical sentences and then try to keep going for a while maintaining the same musical character whilst developing the rhythms:

1. Using short rests on the beat:

2. Using dotted rhythms:

3. Using triplets:

4. Using syncopation:

Things to do

Try teaming up with friends and fellow students to play the following short piece for percussion ensemble. All the parts are played on untuned percussion instruments (you can make your own choices of instrument if you prefer) so there is no melody or harmony in the piece; instead the focus is very much on rhythm.

Hit and Miss – ensemble piece for untuned percussion

Richard Knight

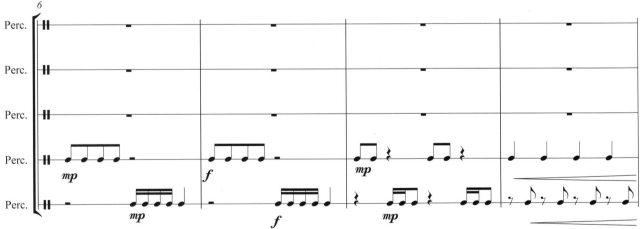

When you have become familiar with the piece, try answering the following questions:

- What is the connection between the start and end of the piece?
- How many musical sentences (or phrases) does the piece have?
- Which musical sentences are the same?
- How complicated is the rhythmic identity of each musical sentence?
- How is the final musical sentence extended and developed?
- In how many bars does one of the instruments play the whole time (i.e. has no rests)?
- How important are the dynamic markings to adding extra interest to the piece?

 ## Composing ideas

Now try your hand at writing your own ensemble piece for untuned percussion. Do not be overly ambitious, but use simple patterns in imaginative ways. Make sure you ask your friends to help play your piece when you have finished.

When, during your course, you meet the more elaborate rhythmic techniques such as hemiola and polyrhythm, try to incorporate them into short pieces for untuned percussion or clapping.

Responding to Harmony and Tonality

The moment a composer moves away from untuned percussion instruments and introduces pitch, it is likely that Harmony and Tonality will be very important. If this element is not controlled, the music is likely to sound rather random and very dissonant. Read through the sections on Tonality and Harmony in the Introduction and especially the part on 'Diatonic Chords' (on page 47).

Traditionally, Roman numerals are used to identify the seven chords available in each key.

It is best to start your exploration of harmony and chords in the context of a major key. The most common chords in a major key are those on the first, fourth and fifth degrees of the scale, known as chord I, chord IV and chord V. All three of these chords will be major. For music in C major, these will be:

C major   F major   G major

These chords are the basis of a lot of music ranging from Mozart to rock and roll and the blues. Try experimenting with them in various orders. One that works quite well is as follows:

I   IV   I   V   IV   I   V   I

A little more variety and subtlety can be provided, without using any other chords, by changing the bass note of some of the chords. In the example above, the bass jumps around a lot between C, F and G. The version below has the same chord pattern, but by using other notes from the chord in the bass (i.e. using the chords in different inversion), this leaping around is ironed out somewhat:

I   IV   Ib   V   IVb   Ic   V   I

Through this method it is possible to organise these three chords into a pattern that fits a bass line that descends in a scale. This is a common feature in music ranging from Bach (e.g. 'Air' from the third orchestral suite – see page 73) to many pop ballads.

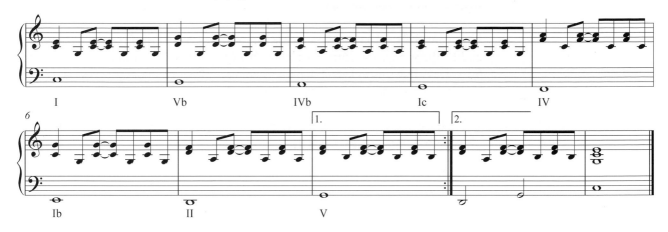

Two things to note:

 In bar 7 this pattern uses, for the first time, one of the other chords in C major: chord II which is a minor chord

 Throughout there is just one chord per bar until the second time bar when the speed of chord change doubles for the final cadence.

Things to do

If you are a keyboard player, experiment with playing this pattern in other keys. Remember: the left hand should be playing a descending scale.

There is one other pattern of chords that is often found in music and this is based on the circle of 5ths which we met on page 41. Remember every step around the circle is a perfect 5th.

Using the circle below, tick every note that belongs to a C major scale:

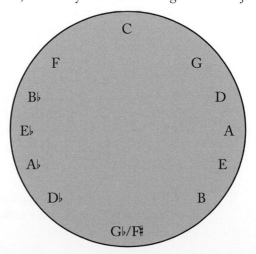

You should have ticked seven of the notes and these seven should be all neighbours on one side of the circle; similarly the five that are left unticked are all together on the opposite side.

Now consider the last notes on either end of the semi-circle of the ticked side: B and F. These, too, are a 5th apart (though a diminished 5th rather than a perfect 5th). This allows us to keep the pattern going without changing key, by using a shortcut across the middle of the circle.

Using these notes as the order for arranging the chords of C major creates a very pleasing harmonic progression:

Once you have put the chords in this order you can, of course, change some of the chords into first or second inversions.

optional notes

Piano

| I | IV | VII | III | VI | II | V | I |
| C major | F major | B diminished | E minor | A minor | D minor | G major | C major |

Listening ideas

Among the songs that rely heavily on this progression are:

- 'Fly Me to the Moon' – Bart Howard
- 'I Will Survive' – Gloria Gaynor.

Responding to Melody and Texture

More often than not we recognise a piece first and foremost by its melody, for it is usually the most noticeable element of a piece (in a song it is the part of the music that carries the all-important lyrics). Read through the section on Melody in the Area of Study section, and especially the passage on melodic contours (page 32).

The direction and energy of a melody is central to its musical character. Melodies which rise (or in which the rising is more noticeable than the falling) are usually more positive than those that fall. The more a melody leaps, rather than moving in conjunct steps, the more intensified the emotion will be. Wide rising leaps seem to stretch outwards and can create a sense of confidence or yearning. Wide falling leaps can add a touch of nobility or even gloom.

Melodies that are mostly conjunct are easier to remember than those that leap the whole time because they are easier to sing.

If you are uncertain how to go about writing your first melody, it can therefore work well to rely on scalic patterns:

Arpeggio-based contours offer a confident character for a melody, since they comprise various leaps, but between a set of pitches that belong together harmonically:

Once you have written a couple of bars of a melody that you like, try to keep the same musical character for much of the remainder of the melody, at least until you reach the start of a new section that you want to make strongly contrasting. It is all too easy for a melody to lose its way after a promising opening few bars.

Composing ideas

There are many ways to design a successful melody. One that you might like to experiment with can be broken down into the following steps:

- Invent a rhythm pattern that lasts for two whole bars. The longest note value should be the last one.
- Now use your rhythm and convert it into a melody. The first note should be the tonic (C); the last note should be the supertonic (D)
- For bars 3–4 use the same rhythm and a similar contour, but different notes and end on the tonic (C)
- Bars 5–6 should be identical to bars 1–2
- Bars 7–8 should again use the same rhythm, but will have different notes: it should end on the dominant (G) and any Fs should be made F♯ (there should be at least one F♯)
- Design a new rhythm for bar 9: it should use a note value not used in bars 1–8
- Convert your new rhythm into a melodic shape; this should include the return of F♮
- Copy bar 9 into bar 10, but move every note either one step higher or one step lower
- Begin bar 11 in the same way as bar 10, moving the notes another step higher or lower; in the second half of the bar go in a new direction and continue into bar 12, ending on the dominant (G)
- Bars 13–14 should be identical to bars 1–2
- Bar 15 should be very similar to bar 3, but with some extra, surprise detail
- Bar 16 should end on the tonic (C).

Before you try this for yourself, you may like to examine the following melody which has been written following these instructions. Check that you can see each step of the process explained above.

Now see what melody you can invent through following these steps.

Texture can often become an element of music that receives little attention from inexperienced composers; yet, with a little imagination, an interesting treatment of texture in the composing process can often bring a piece to life. So read through the section on texture in the Introduction, and make sure you understand what is meant by the texture of a piece of music. Then look at some of the pieces which you know (perhaps the ones you are learning to play) and see what interesting things are done with the texture.

Common weaknesses found in GCSE compositions with regard to texture include:

- No change and contrast of texture
- The melody is automatically assumed to be at the top of the texture for the whole piece
- The same accompaniment pattern is maintained throughout the piece
- All instruments involved in the piece play all the time: there are no rests
- All the notes used are the ones that exist on the treble and bass clef staves, even though the instruments used have many other notes one side or other (or both) of the stave.

Composing ideas

Texture can either be involved in the very first moments of inventing your musical ideas, or it can be considered at a slightly later stage when you have already found some melodic and/or harmonic material for your piece. Either way, the following considerations can be used to bring character and interest to the way you approach texture:

- Could you try doubling your melody in octaves, or even two octaves apart?
- On the second appearance of the melody, could you have an extra descant tune playing above it in the texture, or as a countermelody below?
- Could you have a section in which the melody is in the bass?
- Have you changed the accompaniment pattern at some point, perhaps for the second section?
- Have you included some rests in the texture?
- Are there any opportunities for imitation of a fragment from the melody elsewhere in the texture, perhaps while there is a long note in the melody?
- Could you have a passage in which every note is above middle C to create a bright texture; or below middle C to create a rich texture?

Consider the variety of textures that are used to treat the following single bar of music for piano. All other aspects are the same: every version shares the same melodic shape, the same harmonic progression and the same essential rhythmic character. Listen carefully to what variety is achieved through the five textures.

Responding to Timbre and Dynamics

Whatever you choose to compose, there will, unavoidably, be the need to use some sort of timbre. At a basic level this is reflected in your choice of instrument(s) for playing your composition.

A resourceful response to timbre and dynamics involves more skill and imagination than this, however. In this regard, computers – for all their benefits – can be a disadvantage. Many soundcards make a poor approximation of real instruments (especially strings) and, even where the sound is quite realistic, they do not reflect the variety of tone that each instrument can produce. With acoustic instruments, the following aspects affect timbre:

- The dynamic the instrument is being played
- The part of the instrument's range being used
- The type of articulation being used
- Specialised playing techniques
- Which other instruments are involved in the blend of sound.

The best way to appreciate all these factors is to talk to someone in your school who plays the instrument for which you are writing. Ask them to demonstrate the instrument's capabilities. Then try to remember the sounds you hear when you return to your computer to work on your composition.

Responding to Structure and Form

Fairly early on in the composing process you will need to give thought to how you are going to structure your piece. Without a good control of structure the best musical material can lose its potential effectiveness as the piece drifts from one idea to the next leaving the listener a little bemused: it can become difficult to discern when the end is approaching.

This is where a clear sense of structure is important. The structure of a piece of music is rather like the baking tins for making a cake, into which you pour your cake mixture, and without which you are likely to end up with a mess.

During your class work for Unit 1 you will learn about numerous ways of structuring music. This experience should give you plenty of ideas for how you might handle the structure of your compositions.

Considering structure can work in two opposite directions. You might have invented some good musical ideas and you might then decide upon a structure to suit your material. Alternatively you can take a very detached view to write in, say, Rondo form, and by following the outline of the form you will be steered into thinking of the material you need for each section.

When you get to the start of a new section that is meant to be providing some contrast from what has been happening up to that point, remember that you can achieve that contrast by changing one or more factors of the music: maybe the tempo, the key, the texture or the rhythm patterns. It is unlikely that you will change everything for this will almost certainly generate a new section that seems to belong to a completely different piece to your first section.

UNIT 3: PERFORMING MUSIC

WHAT DOES IT INVOLVE?

This unit requires you to perform as a musician and is worth a considerable 40% of the total GCSE marks. It is important, therefore, that you prepare thoroughly for this unit. There are some general comments about working at your performing in the Introduction section of this guide (page 7).

You are expected to provide recordings of two performances:

■ An individual performance or technology-based performance
■ A group performance.

> Neither performance should last more than 5 minutes.

INDIVIDUAL PERFORMANCES

This option will suit you if you have skills as an instrumentalist or vocalist. Your performances will be assessed by your teacher, and the recording will be sent to AQA for moderation.

An individual performance may either be an unaccompanied solo, such as a piano piece or instrumental study, or it may be an accompanied solo.

Top Tips

It is better to perform music that you can play accurately and confidently rather than attempt something that you find very challenging and will cause you to be nervous. At most, playing a very easy piece will only reduce your potential score by 3 marks – it would be very easy to lose more than 3 marks by attempting a piece that is too difficult for you, as you risk losing marks in all the other categories of the mark scheme: **Accuracy**, **Communication** and **Interpretation**.

■ To score highly for **Accuracy**, all aspects of realising the piece will need to be secure, including pitch, intonation and rhythm.
■ To score highly for **Communication**, you will need to communicate the character of the piece beyond the music stand in front of you and across to your audience; you will need to show that you are involved in the mood of the music.
■ To score highly for **Interpretation**, you will need to show through your playing (or singing) that you appreciate the style of the music; this is reflected in choosing an appropriate tempo, and having good control of the dynamics and other performance directions.

TECHNOLOGY-BASED PERFORMANCES

This option will suit you if you have interest and skills for recording and/or sequencing work. Your task is to produce a performance electronically either using sequencing software or through multi-track recording techniques. You may combine both approaches should you wish.

There is a minimum requirement that the piece you choose must have at least three parts. At least one of these must be performed, by you, in real or step time.

Your work will be assessed on the following aspects:

- Accuracy of pitch and rhythm
- The attention given to expressive details
- Success in producing a good balance between parts
- Use of a good dynamic range
- Control of panning techniques
- Evidence that you have responded appropriately to the style of your chosen music.

GROUP PERFORMANCES

This is a compulsory requirement with no alternative option. Your task here is to perform as part of a group. It is possible to fulfil the board's requirements by playing with one other person; it may suit you better to play in a group of three or four. Should you wish you could play in a much larger ensemble; however, it will be important that your role in the piece is easy to identify so that your contribution to the performance can be assessed fairly.

Once again it will be to your benefit to be playing a part that is above a grade 4 standard, but you should not risk losing lots of other marks just to score highly in this one area. There are only up to 3 marks for the level of difficulty, but up to 9 for each of the other categories: Accuracy, Communication & Interpretation, and Sense of Ensemble.

This final category of marks is significant. Playing in a group requires extra skills to playing a solo piece, and you will need to listen to other members of your group to make sure that you are playing perfectly in time with them (especially at any changes of tempo in the music) and creating a good blend of tone and balance of dynamic with them. If one of your fellow players has the melody at one point, and you only have an inner accompaniment part, you need to play a little quieter.

UNIT 4: COMPOSING MUSIC

What does it involve?

This unit requires you to compose a second piece of music, different from the one required by Unit 2. It is worth 20% of the total GCSE marks.

There is considerable overlap between what is required in Units 2 and 4. The main differences for Unit 4 are:

- There is no Appraisal section in this unit: all the marks are awarded for your composition
- You have up to 25 hours of controlled time to complete your piece
- The piece can be in any style you wish.

Otherwise other aspects are the same as for unit 2:

- You have to provide a score of your piece (which can be staff notation, graphic notation, tab, or a written account of your piece)
- You have to provide a recording of your piece (which can be made after the 25 hours of controlled time has finished if you wish)
- You should set out to explore two or more of the Areas of Study in your piece.

GLOSSARY

Acciaccatura. A melodic ornament where a neighbouring note is sounded for a fraction of a second before the main note of the melody (♪).

Antiphonal. A musical texture in which two groups of musicians take it in turns to play or sing. Originally, the groups would be situated at some distance from each other.

Appoggiatura. A melodic ornament where a neighbouring note (that sounds dissonant) is sounded for a measured period of time before the main note of the melody.

Arco. An instruction for players of bowed string instruments to resume using the bow after a passage of pizzicato playing.

Arpeggio. The result of playing the notes of a standard chord in ascending or descending order.

Binary. A musical structure in which a short piece has two sections, each of which are repeated, with a modulation to a related key at the halfway point.

Blue note. A flattened degree of the scale (usually 3rd, 5th or 7th) popular in jazz and blues styles.

Cadence. A formula of two chords at the end of a phrase that provides a sense of articulation in the music before the next phrase; there are four main types: perfect, plagal, imperfect and interrupted.

Cadenza. An extended passage for the soloist in a concerto, usually unaccompanied and virtuoso. Traditionally the cadenza is a decoration of the cadence at the end of the first movement just before the coda.

Calypso. A traditional style of music from the Caribbean, usually featuring steel pans.

Chamber music. A genre of music for small groups of musicians, such as string quartets, in which each musician plays a unique part.

Chromatic scale. A scale of semitones that includes all 12 pitches commonly used in western music.

Compound time. A metre in which the main beat is sub-divided into three equal portions (cf. simple time).

Concerto. A genre of music featuring a soloist accompanied by orchestra to form a substantial piece, often in three movements.

Conjunct. A style of melodic writing in which each note is a step away from the previous one (cf. disjunct).

Con sordino. An instruction for players of brass and bowed string instruments to play using a mute to create a more restrained and distant sound.

Consonance. A combination of notes that produces a pleasing sound when played together (cf. dissonance).

Continuo. An essential part of instrumental music in the Baroque era comprising a bass instrument (cello, bassoon, etc.) and a harmony instrument (harpsichord, organ, lute, etc.) to provide the backdrop to the rest of the musical texture.

Crescendo. A gradual increase in dynamic (cf. diminuendo).

Cross rhythm. A pattern in which the rhythmic detail of the music is out of phase with the underlying pulse.

Crotchet. A note of quarter of a **semibreve** in duration.

Demisemiquaver. A note of one eighth of a **crotchet** in duration.

Diatonic scale. A major or minor scale; diatonic music will only use notes of the home key.

Diminuendo. A gradual reduction in dynamic (cf. crescendo).

Disjunct. A style of melodic writing including many leaps between one note and the next (cf. conjunct).

Dissonance. A combination of notes that produces a clashing sound when played together (cf. consonance).

Dominant. The fifth degree of a diatonic scale, and the second most important note of any key.

Dotted note. A note value that, by including a dot after the note, is 1½ times its original duration (e.g. a dotted minim is 3 beats long).

Downbeat. The first beat of the bar, traditionally indicated by the conductor's baton moving vertically downwards.

Dynamic. The element of music that relates to how loud it is played.

Flat. The lowering of pitch through use of the ♭ symbol to create a note a semitone lower (cf. sharp).

Fortissimno (*ff*). The dynamic marking for very loud (cf. pianissimo).

Glissando. A playing technique that involves the continual changing of pitch to create a sliding effect from one note to the next (cf. portamento).

Ground bass. A structural device used in Baroque music involving a phrase in the bass that is repeated throughout the piece.

Harmony. The element of music created by notes being played simultaneously, creating a vertical dimension on the stave.

Hemiola. A cross rhythm in triple time in which alternate beats are stressed over the course of two bars instead of every third beat.

Homophonic. A musical texture in which all parts (melody and accompaniment) move in similar rhythm creating a chordal effect.

Interval. The gap in pitch between two notes.

Kora. The traditional harp of music from West Africa, especially Mali.

Leading note. The seventh degree of a diatonic scale, that leads to the tonic.

Legato. A playing style where successive notes are deliberately joined up to create a smooth effect (cf. marcato and staccato).

Major scale. A diatonic scale characterised by semitones between the third and fourth degrees and the seventh and eighth degrees, thereby including a bright 'major' 3rd (cf. minor scale).

Marcato. A playing style in which successive notes are given an extra stress (or 'marking') to bring a degree of attack to the start of each note (cf. legato and staccato).

Mbira. A traditional instrument of sub-Saharan Africa comprising a series of metal prongs that are made to vibrate through flicking them with the fingers.

Mediant. The third degree of a diatonic scale.

Melody. The element of music created by single notes being played successively, creating a horizontal dimension on the stave, commonly known as the tune.

Merengue. A lively style of music from the Dominican Republic in the Caribbean.

Metre. The regularity of stressed beats in the pulse of a piece of music, usually indicated by the time signature.

Minim. A note of half a **semibreve** in duration.

Minor scale. A diatonic scale characterised by semitones between the second and third degrees and the fifth and sixth degrees, thereby including a sombre 'minor' 3rd and 6th (cf. major scale).

Modes. An alternative series of scales to the diatonic major and minor scales used in a variety of styles of music (see page 28).

Modulation. The process of changing key midway through a piece (see page 44).

Mordent. A melodic ornament which involves a move away from the main note to one a step above or below and then returning to the main note again, all in quick time (∿).

Pedal note. A sustained or regularly repeated note, usually heard in the bass while the harmony above changes between various chords. Usually the pedal note is the tonic or dominant.

Pentatonic scale. A scale comprising only five notes (see page 24).

Pianissimo (*pp*). The dynamic marking for very soft (cf. fortissimo).

Pizzicato. An instruction for players of bowed string instruments to play by plucking the string rather than using the bow.

Polyphonic. A musical texture in which two or more parts move independently of each other, creating a layered effect of several different strands.

Portamento. A singing technique of sliding between notes (cf. glissando).

Pulse. A regularly recurring sense of beat common to most styles of music.

Quaver. A note of half a **crotchet** in duration.

Raï. A style of folk music from Algeria.

Reggae. A style of popular music originating in the 1960s in Jamaica in the Caribbean.

Relative keys. A pair of keys, one major the other minor, that share the same key signature; for example, D minor is the relative minor of F major, while F major is the relative major of D minor.

Reverb. A technique used in electronic music to create the sense of the sound originating in a resonant space.

Rhythm. The element of music that controls when notes are played.

Rondo. A musical structure often used in the final movement of sonatas and concertos from the Classical period; a main theme returns on several occasions in the tonic, with contrasting episodes in between.

Semibreve. A note of four **crotchets** in duration.

Semiquaver. A note of quarter of a **crotchet** in duration.

Semitone. The smallest step in pitch available on a keyboard, and the smallest interval in tonal music.

Sequence. A short melodic shape or phrase which is immediately repeated but at a different pitch.

Sharp. The raising of pitch through use of the ♯ symbol to create a note a semitone higher (cf. flat).

Simple time. A metre in which the main beat is sub-divided into two equal portions (cf. compound time).

Sonata. A substantial piece for a solo instrument (or possibly melodic instrument with piano accompaniment) usually in three movements.

Staccato. A playing style where successive notes are deliberately shortened to create a detached effect (cf. marcato and legato).

Subdominant. The fourth degree of a diatonic scale.

Submediant. The sixth degree of a diatonic scale.

Supertonic. The second degree of a diatonic scale.

Syncopation. A rhythmic device in which emphasis is given to a moment that does not fall on the beat.

Tempo. The element of music that controls how fast the pulse beats.

Ternary. A musical structure in which a short piece has three sections, the outer ones being similar and the central one contrasting in some way, usually being in a different key.

Tierce de Picardie. A harmonic device in which a piece in a minor key ends on a major version of the tonic chord.

Timbre. The element of music concerned with the actual sound quality, or tone colour, of the music.

Time signature. The device at the start of the stave that indicates the metre of a piece.

Tonality. The system of 12 major and 12 minor keys.

Tonic. The first degree of a diatonic scale, otherwise known as the key note.

Triad. A chord of three notes built out of two intervals of a 3rd, giving a root, 3rd and 5th to the chord.

Trill. A melodic ornament in which the main notes alternates rapidly with the note above (*tr*).

Vibrato. A performing technique in which the pitch of a note slightly wavers rapidly to give the sound greater vibrancy and resonance.

Whole-tone scale. A scale in which every step is a tone, unlike diatonic and modal scales which include two semitones (cf. chromatic scale).